Contents

Foreword by Trevor Smith   1

About the authors   9

Acknowledgements   10

About the Joseph Rowntree Reform Trust   11

Part 1: Analysis, or what the pollsters say   **12**

Human rights, tolerance and asylum   15

Electoral reform   24

Simulating the results of alternative voting systems in Britain   34

Trust in government   40

Opening up and devolving government   47

British democracy   54

Conclusions   55

Tables

Table 1:   Does Britain need a Bill of Rights to protect the liberty of the individual? (1991–2000)   19

Table 2:   Public attitudes towards protests and governance (October 2000)   21

Table 3:   Alternative voting systems for elections to the House of Commons   25

Table 4:   Seats won in the House of Commons (by party) under alternative electoral systems   35
           and their Deviation from proportionality (1997)

Table 5:   Public perceptions of different sleaze and governance issues as a problem (2000)   41

Table 6:   Public views on different options for handling accusations of serious professional   43
           misconduct by government ministers (1995 and 2000)   48

Table 7:   Public views on when government policy papers should be released (1996)   52

Table 8:   What is the right level for handling employment, transport and similar   53
           issues – regional or national? (2000)

Table 9:   Is government power in Britain too centralised? (2000)   53

Table 10: How much power do people want between elections – and how much   55
           power do they believe they have? (1994–2000)

Figures

Figure 1: What rights should be included in and excluded from a Bill of Rights? (1995 and 2000) 17

Figure 2: How justified are different types of protests? (2000) 20

Figure 3: Public views on which categories of asylum-seekers should be given entry to the UK (2000) 23

Figure 4: How people would vote in an election on electoral reform (1997 and 2000) 29

Figure 5: Regional breakdown of voting in mock referendum on electoral reform (2000) 30

Figure 6: How public responses on electoral reform vary with the questions asked (1992–2000) 32

Figure 7: Should local councils be elected under a proportional voting system (2000) 33

Figure 8: Trust in government ministers and advisory committees on issues of public safety (2000) 44

Figure 9: Public faith in the British system of government (1973–2001) 46

Figure 10: The disclosure of ministerial and official policy papers (2000) 50

Figure 11: Should devolved governments have less or more powers? (2000) 51

Part 2: Poll data, or what the people say 58

List of *State of the Nation* and other Polls 58

List of reports on electoral studies 62

The poll data

Labour's constitutional agenda (1997) 63

Table 1: Labour's constitutional policies 64

UK democracy 66

Table 2: How democratic is Britain? 67

Table 3: Democratic values 68

Table 4: How much power do people want between elections – and how much do they have? 68

The governing system 68

Table 5: Faith in the governing system 69

Table 6: British government is out of date 70

Table 7: Britain needs a more European style of government 70

Table 8:   British government is too centralised   71

Table 9:   Strong versus consensual government   71

Table 10:   Constitutional checks and balances   71

Table 11:   Written constitution   72

Table 12:   Important institutions in Britain   72

The powers and role of the monarchy   73

Table 13:   A more continental monarchy?   73

Table 14:   The Queen's constitutional roles   74

Table 15:   The status of the Church of England   75

The role of Parliament   75

Table 16:   Parliamentary control of the executive   76

Table 17:   Parliamentary performance   76

Table 18:   Fixed-term Parliaments   77

Reform of the House of Lords   77

Table 19:   Support for an elected second chamber   78

Table 20:   Reform options for the House of Lords   78

Table 21:   Who should make law in the new second chamber?   79

Table 22:   An elected or partly elected, partly appointed second chamber?   79

Table 23:   Blocking powers of the second chamber   80

Table 24:   Protecting human rights in the second chamber   81

The role and duties of MPs   81

Table 25:   Who should MPs be loyal to?   81

Table 26:   The duties of MPs   82

Policing the conduct and interests of ministers and MPs   81

Table 27:   The legitimacy of MPs' interests   83

Table 28:   Prohibitions on MPs' activities   84

Table 29:   Making and enforcing the MPs' rule-book   86

Table 30:   Responsibility for the conduct of ministers   86

Table 31:   Ex-ministers' job opportunities   87

Perceptions of sleaze under the Blair government   87

Table 32: What kinds of sleaze are a problem in Britain today?   88

Trust in government and politics   90

Table 33: Trust in government advice   92

Table 34: Choice between government and independent advice   92

Electoral reform   92

Table 35: Proportional representation   93

Table 36: Mock referendum on electoral reform   94

Table 37: Public referendums on electoral reform   94

Table 38: Views on the current voting system   95

Table 39: Public responses to various views on electoral systems   96

Table 40: First-past-the-post and unrepresentative government   96

Table 41: First-past-the-post and single-party government   97

Table 42: Proportional representation in local elections   97

Table 43: Options under different electoral systems   98

Referendums, electoral mandates and electoral power   99

Table 44: Electoral mandates   100

Table 45: Electoral power over government   100

Table 46: Parliament and referendums   101

Table 47: Petitioning for a referendum   101

Table 48: Compulsory voting   102

Funding of political parties and election campaigns   102

Table 49: State funding for parties' election campaigns   102

Table 50: Trade union and corporate funding   103

Table 51: Limits on election spending   103

Coalitions   104

Table 52: Single-party, minority and coalition government   105

Table 53: Public perceptions of a 'hung' parliament before the 1997 election   105

Table 54: What kind of government do people want?   107

Devolution, pre-legislation   108

Table 55: Levels of governance   109

Table 56: Scottish devolution   109

Table 57: Referendum on Scottish assembly with tax and spending powers   110

Table 58: Welsh devolution   110

Table 59: Devolution to Northern Ireland   111

Table 60: Regional government in England   111

Table 61: Regional or national government in England   111

Devolution, post-legislative opinion   112

Table 62: Giving people a choice on elected regional government in England   112

Table 63: Choice between national, regional and local governance on selected issues,   113
           England and by region.

Table 64: Who should make policy in London?   117

Table 65: Who should make policy in Scotland?   117

Table 66: Who should make policy in Wales?   118

The civil service   118

Table 67: Responsibilities of civil servants   119

Table 68: Civil service evidence department   119

Table 69: Civil service whistle-blowing   120

Table 70: Post-service employment opportunities   120

The role of the judiciary   120

Table 71: The use of judges' powers   121

Quangos   122

Table 72: Making quangos more accountable   124

Table 73: Who should run local services   124

Freedom of Information   126

Table 74: Support for a Freedom of Information Act   127

Table 75: Release of cabinet and policy papers   127

Table 76: How long should papers be kept secret   128

Table 77: Policy advice; disclosure vs secrecy 129

Table 78: Who should decide what official papers should be disclosed? 130

Human rights 130

Table 79: Belief in a Bill of Rights 131

Table 80: Weakness of individual citizens' rights 132

Table 81: Protection of rights in Europe and the UK 132

Table 82: Political opinion as a safeguard of rights 133

Table 83: Relying on politicians to protect rights 133

Table 84: Danger to rights from large parliamentary majorities 134

Table 85: What rights should be protected in a Bill of Rights? 134

Table 86: What rights should not be protected in a Bill of Rights? 135

Table 87: Police powers and the right of silence 137

Asylum policy 138

Table 88: Britain's approach to different categories of asylum-seekers 138

Popular protest 140

Table 89: What kinds of protest are justifiable? 140

Table 90: Are protests a legitimate way of expressing popular concerns? 142

Table 91: How should governments respond to protests? 143

The National Health Service 143

Table 92: Giving the NHS a constitution of its own 144

Table 93: How open and consultative is the NHS? 144

Table 94: Patients' power over medical treatment 144

European integration 145

Table 95: Effects of economic and political union 146

Table 96: Predictions on developments in the EU, 1991 146

Table 97: Views on possible developments in Britain's relations with the EU, 1996 147

Foreword

From the mid-1980s onwards, a growing popular reaction to the authoritarian and over-centralised governing style of the Thatcher administration began to emerge. The manner of the introduction of the infamous poll tax and its imposition on Scotland, and then England and Wales a year later, served to coalesce alarm and anger about the way Margaret Thatcher governed and to promote renewed interest in constitutional reform. The decision to test-bed the tax in Scotland re-ignited Scottish nationalism and triggered a wave of popular protest (including a widespread refusal to pay). The following year its arrival in England and Wales provoked further protests, a campaign of refusal and riots.

The widespread hostility to the tax finally killed it off. It also acted as a catalyst to public interest in a series of campaigns for democratic and political renewal which have led directly to the partial constitutional reforms of the Blair government and to the tactical voting that secured its emphatic parliamentary majority in 1997. The Scottish Constitutional Convention, comprising a coalition of churches, trade unions, local authorities, voluntary organisations, and the Labour and Liberal Democrat parties, was created and set the agenda for devolution. Charter88 erupted on to the scene as an influential omnibus pressure group to advocate constitutional reform in general and active citizenship in particular. The already established Freedom of Information Campaign continued its protracted expert mission to win a right of public access to government information and to reform the Official Secrets Act. The short-lived magazine *Samizdat* aimed to cultivate a Lib-Lab 'popular front of the mind', and Tactical Voting 87 sought to encourage Lib-Lab voting habits among the majority of the electorate which did not vote Conservative.

The Joseph Rowntree Reform Trust, a foundation that from its inception in 1904 has avowedly avoided charitable status, pursued a policy of providing funds to most of these and other initiatives for constitutional reform. For example, the Trust gave the *New Statesman* the £5,000 loan with which the magazine launched Charter88. But the Trust simultaneously decided to become proactive by promoting its own projects where it perceived significant gaps. Two major projects were launched – the State of the Nation series of opinion polls and Democratic Audit, both of which have been running successfully for the past decade. (The Joseph Rowntree Charitable Trust, JRRT's sister trust, funds the research and academic work of Democratic Audit, as this can properly be paid from charitable money, while JRRT funds specific inquiries of current political relevance, such as the (Lord) Plant report on the future of the House of Lords.)

This book reports on and summarises the ten-year series of opinion polls in Great Britain commissioned by JRRT under the title, State of the Nation, from 1991 to a major survey in 2000 and a follow-up probe this spring. The questions all bear on constitutional and democratic issues. When we considered the first set of questions in 1991, we had very little knowledge of popular attitudes to democratic issues. It was my view that we had to be bold – we should put crunch questions on major democratic issues to the test of public opinion; we had to repeat them at regular intervals to give us a long-term perspective; and we had to publish the responses, whether they were favourable or unfavourable to the democratic agenda, without flinching. Thus a series of questions have been repeatedly asked through the ten years and have formed the core of all the State of the Nation surveys; other questions were bespoke, being tailored to particular issues that arose, such as the Scott report and first outbreaks of parliamentary sleaze.

There have been five major surveys to date, and a variety of smaller ones on specific subjects. We also draw in this book on an ICM poll on democracy devised for Channel 4 by Patrick Dunleavy and Stuart Weir. In a few cases, we have picked up on questions asked before our series began to gain a stronger over-time view of public opinion.

From the outset, too, we adopted a comparatively innovatory approach to respondents – which I would categorise as being 'citizen-oriented' rather than 'institutional'. For example, what is the point of asking people a flat question, 'Are you in favour of proportional representation?', when large numbers of people do not know what proportional representation is, let alone its purpose or how it may affect public life or that of individual people? Similarly, rather than ask people if they want regional government in England on an abstract institutional plane, why not instead ask them at what level of government – national, regional or local – they would prefer certain kinds of decisions to be taken? This approach relates constitutional issues to people's principles, preferences and experience of life, and avoids asking for their views in a vacuum.

In 1991, we also undertook a wholly innovatory approach to the study of general elections in Great Britain (England, Scotland and Wales). Stuart Weir proposed that we should simulate the results of general elections under various other electoral systems. As ever, the idea is relatively easy, but making it work, as Patrick Dunleavy and Helen Margetts have done for the JRRT, is hard and highly technical work. We ran a trial simulation in 1991 (published in the *Independent on Sunday*), and have since published through Democratic Audit two retrospective 're runs' of the general elections in 1992 and 1997, as well as previews of the elections to the Scottish Parliament and Welsh Assembly; and a simulation of the outcomes of general elections under variants of the AV-Plus electoral systems proposed in the report of the Jenkins Commission on Electoral Reform.

The 1997 study was very influential, as it showed that the Alternative Vote, the system that major Labour Party figures were willing to introduce, would have been even more disproportionate in 1997 than the notoriously disproportionate first-past-the-post system that reformers wished to replace.

The purpose of the State of the Nation reports was threefold. First, to provide detailed feedback to those campaigning groups that loosely comprise the movement for constitutional reform so that they (and the JRRT) could gauge their effectiveness and plan their future activities accordingly, i.e., basic market research. Second, we wished to demonstrate to the political classes in the United Kingdom – politicians, civil servants, opinion-formers, political scientists – that there was a deep strain of public opinion that wished for reforms to bring about a more democratic and modern nation. Successive dissemination of the results of our surveys, we hoped, would influence both opinion-formers and policy-makers to take the case for such reforms more seriously.

Third, we wished to test the conventional assumption that the English, in contrast to the Northern Irish, Scots and Welsh, show little interest in how they are governed. That is to say, to test whether there was some kind of imperial hangover that conditioned the English to eschew public affairs in the way depicted by Rudyard Kipling in his poem *The Puzzler* (1909), composed at the height of Empire' which concluded:

> . . .*And while the Celt is talking from Valencia to Kirkwall,*
> *The English – ah, the English! – don't say anything at all.*

Whatever validity such a stereotype may have had in the past, State of the Nation has consistently demonstrated it is the reverse of English attitudes held today. Successive surveys have revealed that English respondents are as concerned as their compatriots to achieve a more democratic and modern system of government and are equally concerned about the defects of the way they are governed now. On some issues, e.g., faith in the way we are governed, the surveys have recorded increasing levels of concern since the mid-1970s. This and similar trends are analysed in this book and set out in detail in the tables which follow.

But what influence have our polls had? The political classes tend to ignore the striking nature of the findings, on the grounds that such issues may very well command high levels of support on the doorstep or street, but they do not have 'salience' in the public mind, and do not show up in the parties' focus groups. Why, then, policy-makers ask themselves, should we move on issues which are uncertain at best and may not in the end prove popular? Even reform-minded politicians fear that, when put to the test of robust political debate and media interpretation, public support may diminish or evaporate.

Even so, though progress has been far from constant, a good deal has been achieved by the advocates of reform in recent years. No one could gainsay the widespread and organised support for devolution in Scotland, or the need for a pluralist constitutional settlement in Northern Ireland, so devolution in Scotland and Northern Ireland was a political given in 1997. Wales was carried along (just) in the slipstream, and the creation of a Greater London Assembly (with a mayor) was a long-term electoral pledge. In all these cases, there is at least a degree of proportionality in the electoral arrangements. A new, albeit closed, proportional system was introduced for elections to the European Parliament. Most striking of all, the Human Rights Act incorporated the European Convention on Human Rights into British law, making government and all public authorities far more responsive to the people they have to deal with.

But Labour's reforming zeal has been limited, especially where changes might challenge executive power. For example, reform of the House of Lords is limited to the partial eviction of hereditary peers and is set to create a largely appointed second chamber (though our polls showed that most people want an elected second chamber). The new Freedom of Information Act, again in contradiction to public opinion as revealed in our polls, gives ministers and officials absolute rights to suppress much information, and cabinet ministers the final say on what information may be released. The government has reneged on the 1997 Labour manifesto commitment to hold a referendum on electoral reform for the House of Commons in the life of the expiring Parliament, and reform has at best been mothballed, if not buried, for a generation. We have appointed rather than elected new regional bodies in England, Wales, Scotland and Northern Ireland. There have also been some actual reverses, most notably the continuing decline in the influence of the House of Commons and corresponding rise in the autonomy and power of the executive, growth rather than abolition of the unaccountable quango state, a continuing reduction in the role and standing of the civil service, an increase in the politicisation of advice to ministers and government information services, and 'crony' appointees even at the heart of government.

Thus, the task of creating a rational and coherent system of democratic government is a long way from completion. The task of securing further reform cannot be left to Westminster and Whitehall simply because both have a vested interest in manipulating the status quo; only extra-parliamentary campaigning, building on the unrealised public wish for change, as shown by successive State of the Nation polls, can bring about the key reforms required to bring the executive under democratic control. As the brief history of the Blair administration has shown once again, incoming governments, initially committed to a programme of extensive reform, are prone to protect executive and political power, get bogged down by 'events', and become timid. Left to their own devices, they are likely to lapse into the pursuit of non-accountable programmes like the Treasury's pet juggernaut, the Private Finance Initiative (PFI), or the false populism of the quango-ridden NHS renewal plans.

A fundamental flaw of the Blair administration's mode of governing is that the subservience to business interests, the labyrinthine structure of quasi-governance and recourse to such anti-democratic initiatives is seriously shrinking the public realm; local councillors and parliamentarians – particularly so in England – have been consistently sidelined in their legitimate roles of guardians of the public good. The governmental demi-monde of quangos, Task Forces, executive (or First Step) agencies, ad-hoc 'czars', regulators and the privately run series of PFI/PPP schemes may have been appropriate in Byzantium, but is hardly the sort of administrative structure that is consistent with the proper workings of a modern democracy.

Constitutional reform is too easily caricatured as being a form of occupational therapy for political parties when in opposition, or as dinner-table material for the 'chattering classes' or academic nerds. State of the Nation results show that interest in reform stretches far wider – most people in Britain want more power as citizens and more open and accountable government. What must be fostered is a politics that is radical in temper and a constitutionalism that is classical in form.

Finally, it is appropriate that I thank the team that has worked on State of the Nation from the start: Professor Patrick Dunleavy, Dr Helen Margetts and Professor Stuart Weir, whose complementary skills and dedication to political pluralism and constitutional reform have created the valuable archive of public views on democratic issues that this book contains. The JRRT is a collegiate body and my fellow Trustees deserve recognition for their constant support for the polls over the past decade; further, my colleagues on the Charitable Trust have made a significant contribution not only to the electoral polling, but also through their proactive backing for the Democratic Audit, a necessary complement to the State of the Nation series. Thanks are also due to Bob Worcester, of MORI, and Nick Sparrow at ICM, for their interest and expert advice.

Trevor Smith

Lord Smith of Clifton

May 2001

About the authors

Patrick Dunleavy is Professor of Government at the London School of Economics and Professor **Helen Margetts** is Director of the School of Public Policy, University College, London. They have acted as consultants on electoral issues to the Independent Commission on the Voting System (the Jenkins Commission), the Government Office for London, the Royal Commission on the Future of the House of Lords, and Lewisham Council.

Trevor Smith (Lord Smith of Clifton) is Visiting Professor, Universities of York and Portsmouth, former Vice Chancellor of the University of Ulster, and Chairman of the Joseph Rowntree Reform Trust from 1987–99.

Professor Stuart Weir is Director of Democratic Audit and Senior Research Fellow at the University of Essex, and is consultant to International IDEA, the British Council and Department for International Development on democracy and governance. He founded Charter88 in 1998.

Jennifer Smookler, who is now working for Charter88, compiled Part 2 of this book and **Suzy Durston** carried out a preliminary ordering of the questions.

Acknowledgements

Over ten years, we have amassed debts to the large number of people who have suggested ideas for questions and commented on those we have devised, pre-eminent among them members of the Joseph Rowntree Reform Trust. We owe particular thanks to Bob Worcester and Brian Goschalk, of MORI, and Nick Sparrow and Martin Boon, of ICM, and their colleagues for their professional advice. Nick Sparrow has been unfailingly helpful with ideas and phrasing questions. Other polling companies that have tendered for polling contracts have provided a wealth of helpful advice and suggestions in conversation, especially Nick Moon, from NOP, and Simon Orton of BMRB. Simulations of the STV election in 1997 relied on the STV Computer Program designed by David Hill, of the Electoral Reform Society. In 1997, Dr Pippa Norris, from the Kennedy School of Government at Harvard University, kindly gave us basic election data.

Professor Ivor Crewe, Vice Chancellor of the University of Essex, Professor David Sanders, of the Department of Government at Essex, and Professor John Curtice, of the University of Strathclyde, advised us on the phrasing of attitude questions, and the questions for a 'mock' referendum on electoral reform in particular. Various other political scientists have kindly given us advice over the years, among them Professor David Denver (University of Lancaster), Dr Barry Jones (University of Wales) and Professor Brendan O'Leary (LSE). Brendan O'Duffy, (who now lectures at Queen Mary and Westbury College, London) worked with us on the 1997 election report, *Making Votes Count*.

We have relied heavily on the support of the staff and members of both the Joseph Rowntree Reform and Charitable Trusts. In particular we owe special thanks to Lord Shutt of Greetland; Steve Burkeman, former Secretary of the Charitable Trust; and Joy Boaden and Tony Flower, the Reform Trust's Secretary and consultant respectively.

Finally, thanks to Jennifer Smookler, who quarried all the poll reports since 1991 for Part 2 of this book, and to Suzy Durston, who did some valuable preliminary work for her.

Patrick Dunleavy
Helen Margetts
Trevor Smith
Stuart Weir
May 2001

About the Rowntree Reform Trust

The Joseph Rowntree Reform Trust Limited, founded in 1904 by the Liberal Quaker philanthropist, Joseph Rowntree, was deliberately set up as a company which pays tax on its income and is therefore free to give grants for political purposes, to promote political reform and constitutional change. Joseph Rowntree was concerned inter alia with maintaining the purity of elections and the freedom of the press and consequently in the past two decades the main focus of the Trust's grant making has been directed towards these areas. The secretary of the Trust is Ms Joy Boaden, JRRT, Garden House, Water End, York YO3 6LP.

Part one

Analysis,
or what the pollsters say

*We can continue with the over-centralised, secretive and discredited system of government that we have
at present. Or we can change and trust the people to take more control over their own lives.*

Tony Blair, June 1996

The late 1980s and early-to-middle 1990s are now widely seen as a low
period in British political and constitutional history. The excesses of the
governing Conservatives, government secrecy and patronage, various manifestations of sleaze, and costly policy disasters like the poll tax, under valued
privatisations, and BSE, provoked (as Trevor Smith writes in the Foreword)
a profound reaction in the political class and informed circles. But what did
the general public make of what was going on? How far did ordinary
people want to respond to political crisis by introducing the constitutional
changes in the fabric of government that groups like Charter88 and the
Scottish Constitutional Convention were demanding? Trevor Smith, then
chairman of the Joseph Rowntree Reform Trust, and his Trustees decided
that the voices of ordinary citizens should be heard – and thus, the 'State of
the Nation' series of polls was born ten years ago. This book is a record of
the people's views; in Part 1, we analyse the main trends in public opinion;

Part 2 records what the polls have had to say in general.

The evidence of the ten years of polls shows the public has consistently been strongly in favour of constitutional reform; and that, even after the Labour government's major programme of reforms, they want both more complete reforms than those which the government has enacted and reforms on which the government has so far failed to act. The public is in general committed to the principles of accountable government and the separation of powers; to a renunciation of the informality of Britain's old political arrangements; to the adoption of strong legal and formal scrutiny and rules of conduct; to more popular participation in government decision-making; and to the proportional principle in elections. Few people profess to have wide knowledge of constitutional and political affairs or institutions; but they have constantly revealed a basic and consensual grasp of the underlying issues.

In general, the polls from 1991 to 2001 have shown and continue to show:

- 70 per cent support for a written constitution
- overwhelming support for human rights – economic and social rights alongside civil and political rights
- a four to one majority in favour of proportional representation in elections to Parliament in 2000
- more radical proposals for Freedom of Information than the government's recent Act contains
- support for a largely elected second chamber (or House of Lords)
- big majorities for a referendum on electoral reform, for fixed-term

Parliaments, for decentralisation of power, for more accountable quangos
* a strong desire for greater popular power over government decision-making between elections.

At the same time, people show little confidence in the way Britain is governed after a brief rise just after 1997. The trust in government, which Labour promised to restore in 1997, is still absent. Large majorities still do not trust ministers and official advisers to tell them the truth on such issues as genetically-modified crops, British beef and nuclear safety. Most people regard sleaze, cronyism, media manipulation and government favouritism as major problems and they want stronger policing of the conduct of MPs. While most people think that Britain is very or fairly democratic, more than a third (36 per cent) think that Britain is becoming less democratic – though they are balanced by an equal proportion who think that we are becoming more democratic.

The data recording all these views (and many more) over time are set out in Part 2. Here, we set out an analysis largely in the perspective of Labour's constitutional reforms and lapses into more established patterns of governmental and partisan behaviour and the latest large-scale 'State of the Nation' survey, carried out in October 2000. We concentrate on major trends in six areas – human rights and tolerance issues; attitudes towards electoral reform; public trust in government and the governing system; freedom of information; devolution of power; and the quality of democracy in Britain. This means that the analysis does not comment on public attitudes on a variety of other democratic issues, including, for example, the quango state and the role of the judiciary; nor does it necessarily fully cover the issues which we do analyse here.

Human rights and tolerance issues

For many observers, the Human Rights Act is the most important of new Labour's constitutional changes. It is unquestionably the measure which is likely to have the widest and most immediate impacts on the situations of citizens outside the devolution areas. Yet media commentators routinely suggest that the legal codification of rights is a metropolitan elite issue, perhaps artificially prominent because of the exaggerated representation of lawyers in political life, but one relatively remote from the concerns of ordinary people. In particular, the civil liberties emphasis of most campaigning for a Bill of Rights is often seen as having little resonance with British voters. They are widely thought to be markedly less tolerant of dissent, and less zealous in defence of individual freedoms, than the publics in countries like the USA with an established emphasis upon fixed constitutional safeguards, or in liberal democracies with an interrupted history (like Germany, Italy or Greece) where people have tended to be more vigilant about possible new lapses. And immigration and asylum policy has long been seen by nervous political elites of all the main parties as an area (like capital punishment) where British populist attitudes or public opinion influences are likely to be intolerant of outsiders, and hence should be insulated from influencing policy too directly.

The basis for some of these conventional views has always been somewhat hard to fathom. In 1991, the first Rowntree Reform Trust survey asked respondents to look at a list of possible elements of a Bill of Rights and to say for each element whether they would like to see it incorporated into or excluded from such a bill or rights; or neither. At that time, some five rights reached 'consensus' levels of support (defined as a net majority of 70 per cent for inclusion over exclusion of the element) – they were (in order of their ranking) the rights to timely NHS treatment, to a jury trial, to privacy in phone and mail communications, to know what information government holds about you, and to join or not join a trade union. In 1995, responses on these issues slipped below the consensus level, but in general the public view showed essentially little or no change.

But Figure 1 shows a radical increase in support for rights-based thinking among voters at large in 2000, after the Human Rights Act had reached the statute book. If you compare the responses in 1995 and 2000, net support for including all the potential protections increased by at least 10 percentage points, and in about half the items it increased radically by 25 to 35 percentage points. Four new elements passed the 'consensus' test in 2000, most reaching a net 80 per cent level – the right to free assembly for peaceful meetings and demonstrations; the right to equal treatment on entering or leaving the UK, irrespective of race; the right to join a legal strike without losing your job; and the right to practise your religion without state inter-ference. In 1995, the survey showed relatively low support for the right of the press to report on matters of public interest, no doubt reflecting public hostility to the excesses of the tabloid press. However, support for public interest reporting jumped from +40 to +64 per cent, while the proportion of people affirming the right of a defendant to remain silent in court without prejudicing his or her case jumped from +3 in 1995 (when the Conservative government was moving to abolish this right) to +46 per cent in 2000. The

Figure 1: What rights should be included in or excluded from a Bill of Rights?

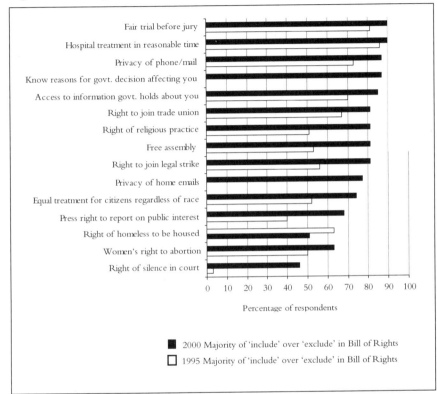

pattern of our responses is also consistent with an ICM survey in March 2000, mainly focusing on NHS issues, which re-used some of these questions.[1] Thus the advent of the Labour government's Act seems to have given British respondents a strong signal in favour of rights-based thinking, with Figure 1 showing that a strong 'rights culture' now exists across the board with consensus or near-consensus levels of support on virtually all elements. The 'Lady Jay myth' that ordinary people care little or nothing for civil liberties issues (she famously told John Mortimer that 'nobody who lives outside the M25 cares about juries') is decisively buried by the fact that 93 per cent of UK citizens (and 98 per cent of Londoners) would include the right to jury trial in a Bill of Rights (2 per cent would exclude it; 5 per cent take no view).

In 2000, we repeated a question that we asked in earlier 'State of the Nation' surveys in 1991 and 1995 – did respondents agree or disagree that Britain needed a Bill of Rights to protect individual liberty? The 2000 responses came in a significantly different context where the incumbent government had just passed the equivalent of a Bill of Rights into law in that parliamentary session, with the Act coming into force just a couple of weeks before our survey date. We might expect, therefore, that some government supporters and others would firm up their views in favour of a Bill of Rights and some government opponents would strengthen contrary views. Table 1 shows that the proportion of people *strongly* agreeing with the need for such protection grew to nearly two-fifths (up from only a quarter in 1991). Supporters of opposition parties did not get more critical of the idea, but net support for a Bill of Rights slipped back slightly because more people gave neutral or 'don't know' responses in 2000 rather than tending to agree. There was an interesting regional variation, with over half of respondents in Scotland strongly agreeing with a Bill of Rights.

Table 1: Does Britain need a Bill of Rights to protect the liberty of the individual? (1991–2000)

	2000	1995	1991
Strongly agree	39	34	25
Tend to agree	32	45	47
Neither agree nor disagree	13	11	–
Tend to disagree	4	6	9
Strongly disagree	3	2	2
Don't know	9	2	7
Net 'strongly agree' minus 'strongly disagree'	*+36*	*+32*	*+23*

Note: In 1991 the responses did not allow 'Neither agree nor disagree'. Hence the italicised bottom row compares only the balance of strongly agree and strongly disagree responses, which are less likely to have been influenced by this change.

The conventional view is that British voters are less tolerant of demonstrations and radical dissent from the established order of things than those in comparable liberal democracies, especially France. This view is believed to reflect a kind of quietist confidence among the public at large that such extravagant behaviours have been unnecessary and hence not fully legitimate in an established liberal democracy like the UK. We had not previously asked specific questions about demonstrations, even though the poll-tax riots may have given us the occasion.

However, 2000 contained very well-publicised incidents of dissent: disruptions of World Trade Organisation meetings in Seattle and Prague; French blockades of ports that inconvenienced many British travellers; the acquittals of Greenpeace protesters who damaged genetically modified crops; prominent May Day demonstrations against capitalism in London; the huge Countryside Alliance march and demonstration against plans to outlaw foxhunting; and in

Voices of the people

Figure 2: How justified are different kinds of protests?

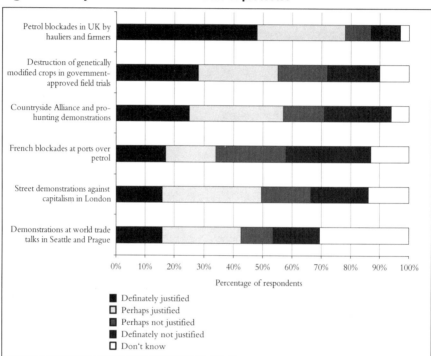

the immediate run-up to our survey, the ad-hoc blockades of oil refineries and petrol supplies which brought the government to the brink of a major internal crisis. So we asked respondents to say how far they thought each of these different kinds of demonstrations or protests was justified. As Figure 2 shows, more than half those polled saw four of the six kinds of protests as definitely or perhaps justified. The UK fuel blockades nearly reached outright approval by a majority of respondents and showed the strongest net majority feeling that they were justified rather than unjustified. We followed up these specific examples of demonstrations with three broader value questions asking people, 'Generally speaking, do you agree or disagree with the following statements?' The responses in Table 2 demonstrate that most respondents followed through their specific endorsement of the fuel protests by giving overwhelming backing to the idea of the legitimacy of peaceful protest. Yet a clear majority also endorsed the idea that general election results should set policy for a full parliamentary term, with less than a quarter dissenting. Opinions were more balanced on whether governments should stand out against protests or demonstrations. These responses show a natural degree of uncertainty in public opinion on the more difficult value questions, but certainly suggest very strongly that, at the time of our survey, public opinion was remarkably supportive of protest actions. Respondents were clearly disinclined to give the Labour government the kind of carte blanche approval for ignoring inter-election opinion which exponents of the manifesto doctrine often claim.

Table 2: Public attitudes towards protests and governance (October 2000)

A   If governments don't listen, peaceful protests, blockades and demonstrations are legitimate ways of expressing people's concerns

B   General election results should set government policy until the next election

C   In a parliamentary democracy, governments should not change policies in response to protests, blockades or demonstrations

	A	B	C
Strongly agree	49	25	13
Tend to agree	32	28	22
Neither agree nor disagree	12	24	26
Tend to disagree	4	14	23
Strongly disagree	3	9	16
Net 'agree' minus 'disagree'	+74	+30	-4

Voices of the people

Public attitudes towards refugees and people seeking asylum in the UK have become politically significant in the wake of increases in the number of asylum seekers in 1999 and 2000 greater in volume than the levels in other major European states like France and Germany. Early in 2000, the Conservative leader William Hague lent his weight to populist tabloid press commentary about 'bogus' asylum-seekers overloading the British system, seeming to elicit a favourable public response in newspaper 'quickie' polls and triggering an apparent toughening of Labour government policy aimed at deterring applicants. Therefore we again introduced a new question in 2000, seeking to tap the public's views in a neutral (non-leading) way, and to gauge in particular the level of public support for the existing British system with its strong emphasis upon case-by-case individual assessment of each application.

For different categories of possible applicants we asked whether respondents believed that the UK should usually allow entry, or usually refuse entry, or judge each case on its merits. Figure 3 shows that the results contradict the notion of intolerant public attitudes, but here again, given that different formulations of questions inevitably shape the public responses in opinion surveys, so the responses of readers in the 'quickie' polls of particular newspapers pursuing strongly hostile editorial policies on asylum will obviously differ from the responses of a wider public to questions which seek to elicit views on the basic principles of asylum policy. In the same way, different survey questions can 'create' differing 'public opinions'. In any event, the 2000 survey provided a neutral base for public consideration of Britain's asylum policy, which a reflective government could build upon in public debate over the aims and outcomes of that policy. In all cases a large

Figure 3: Public views on which categories of asylum-seekers should be given entry to the UK

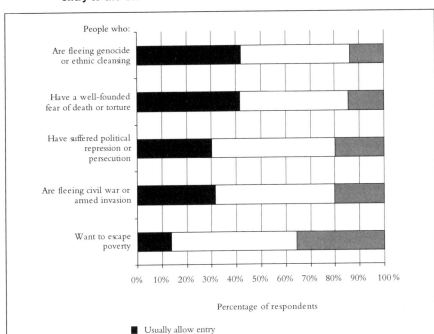

majority of people felt that the UK should either allow entry or judge each case on its merits. Two-fifths of respondents believed that entry should usually be allowed for people fleeing genocide or ethnic cleansing (despite the potential scale of the numbers involved) and for people with a well-founded fear of death or torture (a terminology used in UK legislation itself). Nearly a third of respondents would usually admit people who have suffered political repression or were fleeing civil war or armed invasion (again, despite the likely numbers involved). Only one in eight respondents would usually admit economic refugees whose asylum applications reflected a desire to escape from poverty, but a larger number of people than usual opted for judging this category on the merits of each case. Figure 3 seems to show near-consensus levels of net support for the existing system for the first four humanitarian categories of refugees and asylum-seekers, but much more divided and uncertain public attitudes in the last case. Putting together the response patterns to all the questions reviewed in this section, British public attitudes on rights and tolerance issues seem to be considerably more firmly based on liberal democratic attitudes than most commentators allow. However, political interpretations which, for example, insist that the British asylum system is 'a soft touch', allowing 'hordes' of 'phoney' asylum-seekers into the UK, elicit quite different responses.

Electoral Reform

The unexpectedly large size of Labour's Commons majority in the 1997 general election scuppered whatever scheme for some form of Labour and Liberal Democrat coalition Tony Blair and Paddy Ashdown had discussed. This long-awaited electoral triumph also had a profound effect on Labour Party and trade union activists, and in particular reinforced the hostility of many Labour MPs to electoral reform, as well as greatly increasing the number of hostile MPs, on the simple principle that 'turkeys don't vote for Christmas'. The manifesto pledge for a referendum giving the public a choice between the existing voting system for Westminster and a proportional alternative – first introduced by the late Labour leader John Smith, who was against this particular reform, but genuinely believed that it was an issue which should be decided by the public – became the focus of a determined hostile campaign, led by the AEUW and MPs who did not want to drop the system which had just delivered their remarkable unearned majority in the Commons. Table 3 lists the existing first-past-the-post system alongside its various rivals, including AV-Plus, the hybrid system produced by the Independent Commission on Electoral Reform under Lord Jenkins in 1999.

Table 3:   Alternative voting systems for elections to the House of Commons

Electoral system: *First-past-the-post* (FPTP) is the existing voting system for elections to Westminster. It has essentially been in place since the Middle Ages. People vote in geographical constituencies for a single candidate; and the candidate with the highest vote wins, even if the candidate's vote is lower than 50%.

Type: Majoritarian

Political position: Front-runner in established Labour and trade union circles. Conservatives wish to retain this system too.

Used: Widely used in former British Empire and Commonwealth countries (UK, USA, Canada, India, etc).

Electoral system: Under the *additional member system* (AMS), people vote for half the MPs in local constituencies and cast a party vote for the other half of 'top-up' MPs regionally. A 50:50 split produces a Parliament in which the parties' share of seats closely matches their share of the vote.

Type: Proportional

Political position: Favourite of Labour Party reformers in the Labour Committee for Electoral Reform. First choice of Lord Plant's Labour Party commission on electoral reform, but abandoned under political pressure. Modified AMS system is proving popular in Scotland.

Used: The classic AMS system is used in Germany and New Zealand (which switched from FPTP). Modified versions with lower proportions of top-up seats are used in elections to the Scottish Parliament and Welsh Assembly.

Voices of the people

Electoral system: The *single transferable vote* (STV) gives voters the opportunity to vote for a handful of candidates in large multi-member constituencies – say, for five MPs in constituencies five times larger than current constituencies. Voters are able to express as many preferences as there are candidates and can switch their voters between parties. A pluralist system, but strictly speaking not a PR system and can produce disproportional results.

Type: Preferential

Political position: STV is a British-born creation and has long been the traditional first choice of the Liberals and Liberal Democrats. The short-lived SDP also supported STV. It is also liked by those who dislike political parties and not surprisingly disliked by Labour.

Used: Used in the Republic of Ireland and for elections to the Northern Ireland Assembly and NI elections to the European Parliament.

Electoral system: The *alternative vote* (AV) is a modified version of first-past-the-post voting. People would vote, as now, for MPs in local constituencies, but would be able to indicate second and other preferences which would come into the reckoning in constituencies where no candidate won more than half the votes. Can be even more disproportional than FPTP.

Type: Majoritarian, preferential

Political position: AV is liked by Labour Party figures such as Peter Mandelson as an alternative to PR electoral systems and the nearest alternative to the status-quo.

Used: Used in elections to the lower house in the Australian Parliament and also recently in Samoa where its results led to the political crisis of 1999.

Electoral system: The *supplementary vote* (SV) is a newly created system popular in some Labour Party circles. It is a close cousin of the alternative vote, but restricts the count of second preferences to the two leading candidates in the first ballot if neither wins more than half the votes.

Type: Majoritarian, preferential

Political position: Non-runner for Westminster.

Used: Used for election of London Mayor (by reducing candidates to two for the run-off ballot, SV avoided the confusion of FTPT with a host of candidates and a winner possibly elected on a small minority of the final vote).

26

Electoral system: *AV-Plus* was dreamt up by the Jenkins Commission as a compromise between a majoritarian constituency system like FPTP and a PR system. So it combines AV with a top-up additional member element in a hybrid version of AMS which does not deliver proportionality.

Type: Hybrid

Political position: Designed to be the alternative to FPTP in the referendum on electoral reform to be out to the public before the 2001 election. Reformers have reluctantly rallied round AV-Plus as a move in the right direction.

Used: Untried home-grown system.

Electoral system: Under *List PR* systems, people cast a single vote for a party in very large constituencies, sometimes consisting of the whole country. Most List PR systems are 'closed' – that is, they only give voters a choice between parties, but some 'open' list systems allow a degree of choice of candidates. Thus the parties usually have a decisive say in who their MPs will be by giving favoured candidates the top spots on the party list. Proportionality can vary considerably depending on the counting system used.

Type: Proportional

Political position: Too far in spirit from the traditions of direct constituency representation in British politics to be a serious contender for parliamentary elections here.

Used: List PR systems are used largely in Europe's liberal democracies and for elections in EU states to the European Parliament. Jack Straw chose a closed List PR system for Britain's Euro-elections from 1999 onwards.

The Jenkins Commission created AV-Plus as a compromise between the existing system and a fully proportional alternative.[2] It was controversial inside the Cabinet, the Parliamentary Labour Party and the large trade unions. Labour proponents of electoral reform had to fight hard to save the proposal to keep the referendum pledge as an item in the 2001 election manifesto. In the meantime, however, the creation of the Scottish Parliament, National Assembly for Wales and Greater London Assembly provided an opportunity to introduce new Additional Member System (AMS) methods of voting, marking a decisive break with Britain's past blanket adherence to plurality rule voting. These are variants of the German AMS system, but are less proportional; seats in the German system are allocated on the basis of half to members elected in constituencies, half to 'top-up' members elected from regional party lists to provide a more proportional result than constituency elections alone would produce. The proportion of balancing top-up seats is less than 50 per cent in Scotland (where it is 43 per cent), Wales (33 per cent) and for the Greater London Assembly (44 per cent).

In 1997 we held a 'mock' referendum on electoral reform for general elections. We asked almost 9,000 respondents in an immediate post-election ICM survey to choose how they would vote in a referendum on changing Westminster's voting system, giving them a choice between two options on a showcard that gave short descriptions of the existing voting system or a

Mock referendum showcard

The existing system of voting	A proportional system of voting
• You have a single vote for one MP in your local constituency as now • The two larger parties usually get a larger share of the SEATS in the House of Commons than their share of the national vote • Elections are more likely to produce a government formed by one party	• You have two votes: one vote for an MP in a local constituency somewhat larger than now, and one vote to elect additional MPs for your region • Each party's share of the SEATS in the House of Commons more closely reflects their share of the national vote • Elections are more likely to produce a government formed by a coalition of parties

'mixed' AMS system. We checked the description with a small panel of political scientists to ensure that they were as impartial as we could make them. At that time, as Figure 4 shows, respondents split almost evenly, with just over two-fifths backing AMS and the status quo.

We decided to repeat the mock referendum in 2000, on the basis that the description of the alternative AMS system broadly also described the Jenkins Commission's alternative, AV-Plus. This time a clear majority of respondents opted for change (by 53 to 27 per cent).

There were important regional variations in the 2000 mock referendum.

Figure 4: How people would vote in a referendum on electoral reform, 1997 and 2000

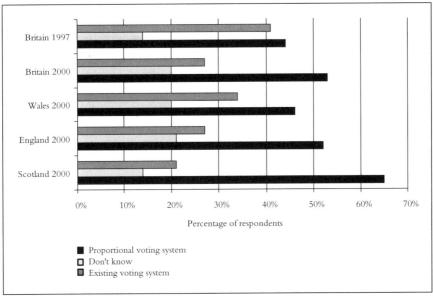

29

Voices of the people

In Wales, the lead for reform was just 12 per cent, but in England it was 25 per cent and in Scotland 44 per cent. Among our small sample in London there was a small majority for the status quo, of 10 per cent. Comparison of the vote for reform in Scotland in 1997 (46 per cent) and 2000 (65 per cent) – from under half to two-thirds of respondents – suggests that the experience of voting under the AMS system for the Scottish Parliament has made

Figure 5: Regional breakdown of voting in mock referendum on electoral reform, 2000

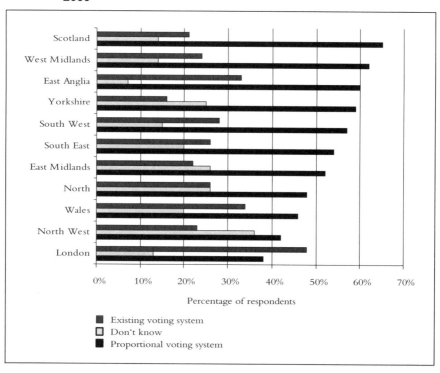

proportional representation more popular and that it has secured wide acceptance in Scotland. But in London and (to a lesser extent) in Wales, the experience with AMS elections has not had a similar popularising effect. Figure 5 sets out the responses across Scotland, Wales and official regions within England. We need to interpret the results cautiously, since our regional samples were small in number. But in six regions there was an absolute majority of support for a change of the voting system, and London was the only case where more respondents said that they would retain the existing system over an AMS alternative. Taken together these results suggest a considerable shift towards acceptance of PR voting between 1997 and 2000, with especially noticeable (but perhaps not long-lasting) willingness among Conservative supporters to envisage supporting reform.

Popular support for proportional representation has been broadly constant at between 56 and 60 per cent between 1992 and 2000 (with a dip to 54 per cent in 1995). In 2000, we also asked a number of other questions which suggested significant public pressure still existed for reforming Parliamentary elections. Asked to agree or disagree that 'A referendum should be held on changing the system we use to elect MPs', 56 per cent for of respondents agreed and only 15 per cent disagreed. Respondents also supported (by 60 to 13 per cent) fixing the length of Parliaments and removing the Prime Minister's power to choose the date of the next election. (In 2001, there was a slight dip to a two-to-one majority for fixed-term elections, with 50 per cent for and 25 per cent against.)

However, we recognise that it is very difficult to get an accurate fix on public opinion on prospective changes like electoral reform which have not yet been fully debated by the political parties and mass media. Earlier surveys in the 'State of the Nation' series have always shown that when respondents are given differently skewed value questions their agree/disagree responses do show substantial changes, suggesting that relatively large numbers of them have uncommitted views susceptible to being influenced by different pro- and anti-reform arguments. Figure 6 shows that this pattern continued in 2000. The first value question here is slanted towards reform and alerts respondents to treating parties fairly, showing a strengthening majority for

Figure 6: How public responses on electoral reform vary with the questions asked

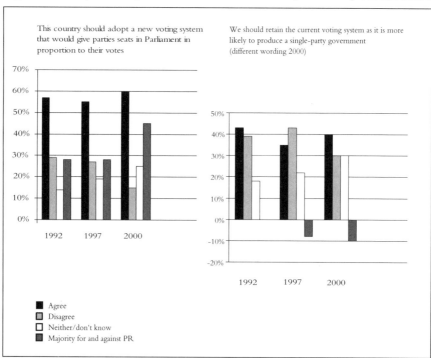

reform since 1992. But the second question is slanted against reform and alerts respondents to retaining single-party government, producing a larger negative balance against PR in 2000 than in earlier surveys.

In 2000, we also investigated people's views on reforming local government elections. This is currently an issue on which Labour and Liberal Democrat discussions on future co-operation between their parties are focused. In Scotland, working party proposals for a shift to the Single Transferable Vote for elections to local authorities (and other reforms) have

Figure 7: Should local councils be elected under a proportional voting system?

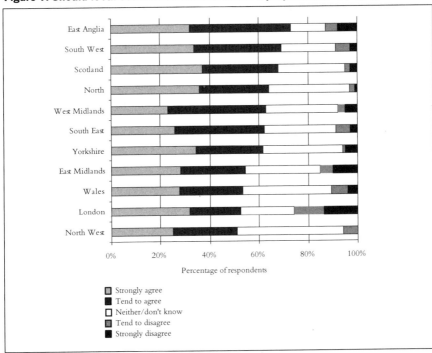

provoked a major backlash in the Labour Party's ranks. This is an issue that could break the ruling Lib–Lab coalition in Scotland, since the Liberal Democrats regard this as a touchstone issue. Yet the public seems to be unmoved by the varying demands of party advantage; as Figure 7 shows, across Britain respondents agreed by 61 to 10 per cent that council elections should be held by PR, with stronger support in Scotland, the South West and East Anglia, and lower (but still majority) support in the East Midlands, Wales and London, and a large number of neutral or don't know responses in the North West. These results suggest that there is little or no strong support for retaining first-past-the-post elections for local councils in most regions, and that a commitment to reform here would enjoy widespread support.

Simulating the results of alternative voting systems in Britain

As Trevor Smith explains in the Foreword, we have not only tested people's views on proportional representation, we have put PR and other alternative electoral systems to the test of 're-run', or mock, elections in 1992 and 1997. Both these 're-run' elections were carried out by ICM Research in Great Britain (excluding Northern Ireland), immediately after the general elections in 1992 and 1997. Respondents in large-scale opinion surveys were asked to 'vote' again on the kind of ballot papers used for the main alternative electoral systems: the additional member system; the alternative vote; the single transferable vote; and the supplementary vote. The results of List PR elections, using three different counting rules, were calculated from the actual election results. These results are simulations and could not of course take account of the political dynamics which would come into play with a new voting system. The tables of 'ballot' results are very complex and we are not able to replicate them here; however, we reported fully on them in *Making Votes Count* (available from Democratic Audit, University of Essex) in September 1997 and they are to be found in the ICM reports (see Part 2).

When the Jenkins Commission report advocated a new voting system, AV-Plus (see Table 3), we carried out further research which enabled us also to calculate the results of an AV-Plus election under the three options that the Commission offered – a 15, 17.5 and 20 per cent 'top-up' (see Making Votes Count 2, also available from Democratic Audit). In Table 4, we set out how many seats the parties would have won in the House of Commons in 1997 under the main alternative voting systems, including AV-Plus.

Table 4: Seats won in the House of Commons (by party) under alternative electoral systems in 1997 and their Deviation from Proportionality (DV)

Voting System (ranked in order of DV score)	Con	Lab	Lib	Nat	Other	DV%
Alternative (and supplementary) vote	110	436	84	10	1	23.5
First-past-the-post	165	419	46	10	1	21
AV-Plus (with 15% top-up seats)	160	378	89	13	1	14.6
Single transferable vote	144	342	131	24	0	13.5
AV-Plus (17.5% top-up)	167	367	92	14	1	12.9
AV-Plus (20% top-up)	175	359	91	15	1	11.6
List PR (D'Hondt rules)★	205	345	72	18	1	10
List PR (Droop rules)★	212	320	89	19	1	7.5
List PR (Hare rules)★	205	295	121	19	1	4
AMS (German version, with 50% top-up seats)	203	303	115	20	0	2
Pure proportionality	202	285	110	16	28	–

★ D'Hondt, Droop and Hare are three of the better-known counting formulae used in calculating the quota of votes required before a party is awarded a seat. They have different effects – for example, the D'Hondt formula, chosen for Euro-elections in Britain, favours large parties. See Making Votes Count, (Democratic Audit 1997), and for a fuller account, R. Taagepera and M. Shugart, Seats and Votes, (Yale University Press, 1989, p.30–2, 274).

Thus, in 1997, Labour would have won a majority in elections under the alternative vote (AV), the single transferable vote (STV) and the supplementary vote (SV) systems. Both AV and SV gave Labour an even greater majority than under the existing first-past-the-post system. STV would have given Labour a smaller overall majority of 44 seats in Great Britain. Labour would have remained the largest party in the Commons under the additional member system (AMS), but Tony Blair would probably have lost his overall majority. The Conservatives got fewer Commons seats in the actual 1997 election than their share of the votes warranted. They would have been much more severely under represented under AV or SV, falling to just 110 seats. Under STV, they would have gained only 144 seats as against the 165 they actually took in 1997. The Liberal Democrats would have taken 84 seats under AV or SV, nearly twice as many as they won in 1997 (46), and 130 seats under STV – nearly three times as many as their share of the 1997 vote warranted.

Deviation from proportionality in our first-past-the-post elections for Westminster has been among the largest recorded – that is, most disproportional – among all liberal democracies for the last 25 years. The lower the figure for deviation (the DV score) in Table 4, the more proportional a system is. Western European democracies using PR systems commonly achieve DV scores of 4–8 per cent – a level only briefly recorded in Britain during the two-party era of the 1950s. In the USA, the solid two-party system in Congressional elections produces stable DV scores of about 7 per cent. So the existing electoral system is broadly three times worse at translating votes into seats accurately than the voting systems in the main countries with whom we usually compare ourselves. These national DV scores for the UK, however, tell only half the story. Higher deviation scores in the regions are hidden from sight by the national DV figure because areas of pro-Conservative and pro-Labour deviation offset each other. In 1997, for example, the national DV score was 21 per cent – which means that the votes of one in five electors in Britain were ignored by the existing voting system. But in 11 out of the 18 regions, DV scores varied from 26 to 42 per cent.

The 21 per cent DV score for the 1997 Parliamentary election can be simply understood as the proportion of MPs who were not entitled to their seats in the legislature in terms of their party's national share of the vote. In other words, after 1997, one in five (21 per cent) of all MPs were not entitled to their seats. Under the classic 50:50 AMS system, only 2 per cent of MPs would have been similarly placed.

But what of rival systems? Prior to 1997, it was widely (though wrong-headedly) believed that the alternative and supplementary vote systems were more moderate versions of first-past-the-post, producing both majorities for the eventual winner in each constituency and less disproportional results overall. In 1992, both would have produced marginally more proportional results than the existing system; in 1997, they would have given even less proportional results than first-past-the-post. STV is generally regarded as a proportional system. These studies tested an STV system of 134 mostly five-member constituencies twice – in 1992 and 1997. The results of the 1992 STV ballot were mildly disproportional. The 1997 results were strongly disproportional – producing a high deviation from proportionality score of 13 per cent. The explanation for the 1997 results is clear. AV, SV and STV are all 'preferential' systems – that is, they allow voters to express more than one preference when they vote. In 1997, people were disillusioned with the Conservatives and reassured by New Labour's moderate image. Voters' second and later preferences reflected the disillusion with the Tories and magnified its electoral effects. In 1997, Labour would have benefited under any of the three systems had they been in operation. Any future government, however, could plumb the depths of political unpopularity (as Labour did in the mid-1980s) and suffer equally punishing results. The single transferable vote is evidently more proportional than first-past-the-post, but the system ought now to be regarded as contingently proportional – that is, as a system which will usually produce fairly proportional results on people's first preferences, but not invariably. None of these systems incorporates a mechanism to ensure that they produce a proportional outcome. The analysis also shows that List PR elections are not necessarily proportional under British conditions. In 1997, for example, Labour's lead over the Conservatives would have varied between 90 seats (under one formula) to 140 (under another), with DV scores ranging from 4 to 10 per cent.

One of the purposes of AV-Plus was to allow for a party to win an overall Commons majority on a minority of the vote in exceptional years, such as 1945, 1979 and 1997. As Table 4 shows, it would have performed this task admirably in 1997, whichever of the three 'top-up' scenarios was employed. However, as a result, it also produces disproportional results under any of these scenarios, as the final column of the table shows. In closer elections, as in 1992, AV-Plus would be nearly proportional, and coalition governments could result. In years when the electorate has reached a decisive view about the need for a change in government, AV-Plus would cut back the unwon landslide Parliamentary majorities which voters dislike and which make a mockery of the idea of opposition in the Commons. But it would still allow for single-party governments whenever a party gains around 44-45 per cent of the vote with a strong lead over the second-placed party.

Overall, the alternative vote (and SV), AV-Plus under the three scenarios, STV and List PR under D'Hondt rules all had DV scores above the broad European norm. As in our 1992 simulation, AMS was the most proportional system, with a 50:50 split between constituency and top-up MPs. As stated above, the classic 50:50 AMS system produces nearly pure proportional results. Had the version of AMS in use in Scotland (with a 57:43 per cent split between constituency and top-up MSPs) been used nationwide in 1997, it would have produced a deviation score of 6 per cent. The AMS variant approved for elections to the National Assembly for Wales (ratio 66:33 per cent) would have produced a quite high deviation score of 9 per cent throughout Britain in 1997.

In 1997, we also asked the 'voters' under alternative systems whether they liked or disliked the systems under which they 'voted'. There were two-to-one majorities in favour both of the additional member system and the supplementary vote, both of which retain voting with an X. But people were almost evenly divided for and against the alternative vote, and strongly disliked the more complex STV ballot paper. Interviewers also asked people whether they would prefer one MP to represent the area they lived in or several MPs, possibly from different parties, to represent a larger area. Those who chose the single-constituency MP outnumbered those who wanted several MPs by more than two to one. In February 1998, we tested two versions of the List PR system to be used in the Euro-elections – one with an 'open' list, which allowed voters to choose between candidates as well as parties, the other 'closed', allowing a party vote only. There was a small majority – 51 to 46 per cent – in favour of 'open' list voting. The professional and managerial class particularly preferred open voting, splitting 58 to 40 per cent between the two options. Two-thirds of voters were positive about voting on List PR ballot papers.

Trust in Government

Confidence in the Major government crumbled under widespread perceptions of 'sleaze', a portmanteau term which allowed the media to roll up a variety of phenomena – patronage, bribery, interest group lobbying of MPs, political appointments to quangos, and even the spread of the quango state itself. Major worked hard to restore faith in government, for example, through establishing a Committee for Standards in Public Life and creating a tougher supervisory regime for MPs' interests. Labour was still able to exploit 'sleaze' issues up to and during the 1997 election and came to power with a commitment to regain the public's trust in government in general and an implicit pledge to shift towards a responsive 'people's' government and away from the governing style and institutional arrangements which they inherited from the Conservatives.

However, 'sleaze' has not gone away as an issue, partly due to the Conservatives' determination to exploit cases like that of the business career of the former Paymaster General Geoffrey Robinson, Tony Blair's alleged 'cronyism', the 'Lobbygate' affair, and so on. In 2000, we therefore asked some questions designed to determine the extent of public confidence that new Labour had managed (or not) to instil in the people. Table 5 shows how people responded to a number of different issues to the question:

'Thinking about Britain today, do you think that each of the following is a major problem, a minor problem, or not a problem at all?' In each case, half or more of respondents answered that the issue in question was a major problem, with a pattern of responses showing some partisan alignment. For instance, 65 per cent of Conservative supporters saw ministers favouring large private interests over ordinary people as a major problem, compared to around 60 per cent of nationalist and Liberal Democrat supporters, but also over half of Labour supporters.

Table 5: Public perceptions of different sleaze and governance issues as a problem (%)

A   Government ministers not being truthful
B   Government ministers favouring major private interests over the interests of ordinary people
C   The government using spin-doctors to manipulate the media
D   Ministers appointing to government committees and task forces people who have made large donations to their party
E   The granting of peerages and honours to people who have made large financial donations to political parties
F   Ministers appointing friends to important public posts
G   Financial sleaze in government

	A	B	C	D	E	F	G
Major problem	66	58	57	52	52	50	49
Minor problem	26	29	30	35	32	36	39
Not a problem at all	4	6	5	6	8	7	6
Don't know	5	6	8	6	8	7	6

In 2000, we also turned again to a set of questions we first asked in 1995 to tap respondents' attitudes about the conduct of MPs in relation to earning money from lobbying and other activities. In 1995, we found high levels of public disquiet and dissatisfaction with the system for checking misconduct. We modified the same questions in 2000, with a small change to the preamble to recognise the post-Nolan role of the Commissioner for Standards. We found that the public response was largely unchanged – respondents still wished to make the rules governing MPs into law and to introduce external regulation of MPs' conduct (63 per cent) rather than allow the current system to continue (28 per cent). As we write, there are persistent rumours that MPs' dissatisfaction with the rigour of the incumbent Commissioner, Mrs Elizabeth Filkin, is so strong that her contract may not be renewed when it comes up for renewal in January 2002. MPs may wish to consider the adverse impact such a move is likely to have on public confidence in their role.

In the light of the series of embarrassments for the Labour government involving ministers, such as the resignations of Peter Mandelson, Geoffrey Robinson and Ron Davies at Westminster, and other cases in Scotland, we also repeated another 1995 question: 'How do you think accusations of serious professional misconduct by government ministers should be investigated?' Table 6 shows the striking consistency in public responses between 1995 and 2000, with only a tiny growth of confidence in the capacity of the House of Commons to investigate the behaviour of ministers. The vast majority of respondents in both years insisted on an external inquiry, with only one in ten people or less endorsing the status quo with the Prime Minister alone responsible for judging the conduct of ministers.

Table 6: Public views on different options for handling accusations of serious professional misconduct by government ministers (1995 and 2000)

A   An independent official commission should investigate and decide whether ministers should resign

B   The police should investigate and decide whether or not ministers should face legal trial in court.

C   The House of Commons should make enquiries and decide if the minister should resign

D   The Prime Minister should make enquiries, as now, into whether allegations are true and decide if the minister should resign

E   Don't know

	A	B	C	D	E
2000	42	28	16	7	8
1995	47	31	12	11	3

One major area of public distrust in the 1990s, epitomised for the bulk of people by the BSE tragedy, concerned official advice from government ministers and their advisers on issues of food safety, technological change and industrial regulation – an area of modern politics which some influential commentators have argued has become increasingly critical. The continuing series of deaths from BSE and the review of government policy towards the crisis by the Phillips inquiry combined with acute controversies over the introduction of genetically modified (GM) foods and nuclear power stations in Scotland to make such 'risk' issues very prominent in the political agenda from 1997 to 2000. A 'State of the Nation' poll in 1996 suggested low and perhaps declining public faith in government advice on these risk issues, with some suggestion that people trust environmentalist groups more than official spokespersons. We followed up the 1996 questions in 2000, asking again: 'Do you trust government ministers and their advisory committees to tell the truth about each of the following or not?' Figure 8

Voices of the people

shows the results. There are clearly two groups of issues here, with much higher levels of public trust in AIDs and safe sex advice (undoubtedly a tribute to the very careful management of government credibility and engagement of external groups in shaping advice) and almost as high in the safety of medicines. But public confidence on the three other issues – the safety of food, GM crops and foods, and nuclear installations – was at rock

Figure 8: Trust in government ministers and advisory committees on issues of public safety

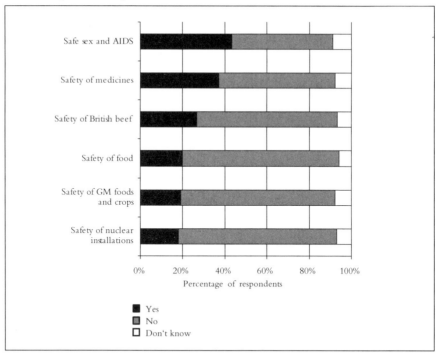

bottom, with less than one respondent in five expressing trust, and three and a half times as many withholding trust. Confidence in government truth-telling about British beef is a little higher, but still shows a massive majority of sceptics.

Taken together, these results suggest that the Labour government did not succeed in its first term in excising substantial public cynicism about the British style of governance.

The public may not trust ministers and politicians, but it shows evidence of more faith in governing arrangements. In 1991, we identified a valuable window into public faith in the system – a question first asked in 1973 for a survey for the Kilbrandon Commission. We (and MORI) have repeated the question with identical wording throughout the 1990s, as well as in 2000 and 2001. The question asked was: 'Which of the following statements best describes your opinion on the present system of governing Britain?' And the responses offered are: 'It works extremely well and could not be improved'; 'It could be improved in small ways but mainly works well'; 'It could be improved quite a lot'; and 'It needs a great deal of improvement'. As very few people have ever in fact endorsed the view that there is no need for improvement, we combine these respondents with those who acknowledge a need for small improvements into a large 'works well' category. Figure 9 shows the very pronounced slump in the proportion of people giving a 'works well' response, from half of the 1973 sample to less than a quarter in 1995, and the parallel rise in those seeing the need for a 'great deal of improvement' from barely one in eleven in 1973 to over a third in 1995. The figure also shows that a MORI poll in April 1998 recorded what seemed like a dramatic turn-around in the public attitude under Labour. The

Figure 9: Public faith in the British system of government, 1973–2001

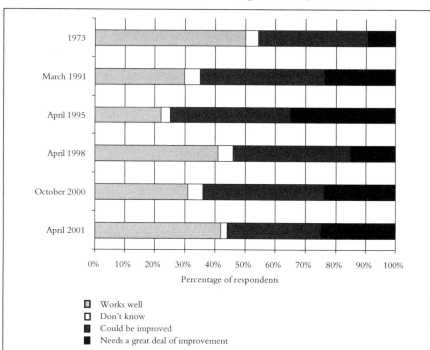

percentage of respondents giving 'works well' responses doubled and those seeing a need for radical improvements halved. Since then, public attitudes have see-sawed, with 'works well' responses falling back in 2000 to below a third, and then recovering again to 1998 levels. Overall, however, the public's view on how well we are governed is not now as bad as in the mid-1990s, but more people still see the need for improvement (56 per cent) than are broadly satisfied (42 per cent).

Finally, the public reveals a desire for clear rules for government ministers and politicians in general. Agreement with the proposition that 'Britain needs a written constitution, providing clear legal rules within which government ministers and civil servants are forced to operate', has been at consensus levels since 1995; and while there has been a gradual fall in backing for a written constitution between 1995 and 2000 (from 77 to 71 per cent agreeing), the number of those 'agreeing strongly' has stood up over time (it was at 37 per cent in 1995; 38 per cent in 2000).

Opening Up and Devolving Government

Two major aspects of Labour's promise of more open government closer to the people were their manifesto commitments to a Freedom of Information Act and devolution. In our pre-election poll in 1996, we found that some three-quarters of the public approved of the pledge on freedom of information, an issue on which there has long been consensus-level support. However, while a majority of people have also long backed proposals for devolution in general, only 40 per cent of respondents across Britain as a whole expressed support for a Scottish parliament, and opinions on the proposal for a Welsh assembly were almost evenly divided (36 per cent for, 34 per cent against). There was a high level of people saying that they did not know – with a large minority of 30 per cent 'don't knows' on the Welsh assembly, 27 per cent in respect of the Scottish parliament.

A switch from the British government's traditional stance of excessive secrecy through a Freedom of Information Act (FOIA) was not only a popular reform, but also a potentially valuable step towards rebuilding public confidence in the way we are governed. Agreement with the proposal for an FOIA, 'giving the right of access to information collected by public authorities, subject to adequate safeguards on national security, crime prevention and personal privacy' was unvaryingly high in four polls from 1991 to 2000 at 77 to 81 per cent. Moreover, people also backed a radical measure; in 1996, 78 per cent agreed that both 'background papers relating to government decisions' and 'civil service papers on government decisions' should be released sooner than any 30-year embargo, and 74 per cent agreed that cabinet papers too should be made public earlier. When asked when such official information should be released, a majority of people said either immediately or after the following general election.

Table 7: Public views on when government policy papers should be released (1996)

In your view, how long do you think papers relating to government decisions should be kept secret?

A Background policy papers
B Civil service advice papers
C cabinet papers

	A	B	C
For 20 years	4	2	5
For 10 years	26	23	22
Until after the next general election	21	21	23
For 1 year	12	14	14
Should be released immediately	34	38	35
Don't know	3	2	2

We followed up on the issue of freedom of information in 2000 and 2001. While the FOIA was still going through Parliament in 2000 with opposition MPs and peers – and some Labour members in both Houses – seeking to liberalise the Act that the Home Office had produced, we asked respondents about two particular hot topics: should the policy advice given by civil servants to ministers be kept secret (as the minister Jack Straw was insisting); and should ministers and senior civil servants acting alone be able to decide what government papers are released (again as the government intended); or alternatively, should an independent commission be able to review the decisions of ministers and officials and order papers to be released in the public interest? The question wording ran: 'Parliament has been debating options for a new Freedom of Information Act. Which of the following options would you yourself prefer?' Figure 10 shows that respondents were strongly in favour of greater openness. By some 79 to 9 per cent, they chose the option of giving an independent commission the power to decide what official papers should be released rather than leaving it to ministerial discretion; and by 68 to 17 per cent, chose the proposition that civil servants' policy advice to ministers should 'normally' be disclosed rather than 'normally' kept secret.

The final Act was amended to restrict the power to overrule the Independent Commissioner on Information to cabinet ministers. So in April 2001, we put the amended position to the public, asking whether cabinet ministers, as in the FOIA, or the Commissioner should have the final say on whether information should be disclosed or kept secret. Some two-thirds (67 per cent) chose to give the Commissioner the 'final say'; less than one in five opted for a ministerial veto. The 'don't knows' were high, at 16 per cent. Overall, it seems unlikely that Labour's FOIA will be seen as doing enough to reduce government secrecy.

Figure 10: The disclosure of ministerial and official policy papers (2000)

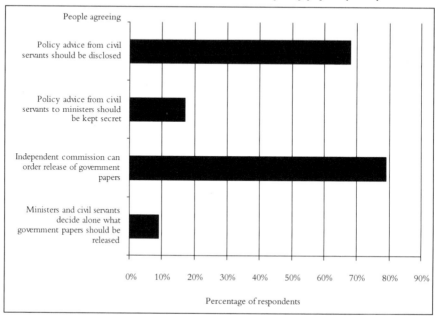

Among the government's reforms, devolution is one of the most important and far-reaching. Part 2 sets out past levels of support for devolution and here we concentrate on the public verdicts in 2000 on the government's actual devolution settlements in Scotland, Wales and Greater London, and inquire into the 'English question'. Some stirrings of support for elected regional assemblies were becoming evident in the English regions after a prolonged post-1997 hiatus. In each of the established areas of devolution we asked respondents: 'Thinking now about [Scotland], which of the following options do you think is the best way of deciding to run health, education and other services, how to generate new jobs, develop major roads and public transport, and other similar issues?' The response options were: 'Give more powers to the [Scottish Parliament and executive]'; 'Keep the powers of government ministers, Whitehall and the [Scottish Parliament and executive] as they are now'; or 'Increase the powers of government ministers and Whitehall'. Figure 11 shows that there was very strong support in Scotland for extending the scope of devolved government, and virtually no backing for taking decision-making back to London. In London, more respondents favoured expanding

Figure 11: Should devolved governments have more or less powers?

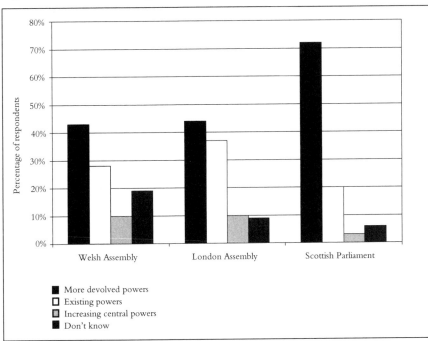

GLA powers than sticking with the status quo, and only one person in ten favoured stronger powers for ministers and Whitehall. In Wales there were a lot of don't know responses, which reduced support for the status quo, but increasing powers again emerged as much the most popular response.

Table 8: **What is the right level for handling employment, transport and similar issues – regional or national? (October 2000)**

	England all respondents	North	East Midlands	South East
An elected assembly for this region should decide	32	43	24	34
Appointed business and local government representatives for this region should decide	29	15	39	25
Government officials meeting at regional level should decide	15	9	23	14
Government ministers in Whitehall should decide, taking into account the needs of the country as a whole	12	16	6	13
Don't know	14	17	10	15

In the English regions, we asked all respondents a general question on similar lines specifically about their region (although the numbers of respondents per region are small). Table 9 sets out the response options and patterns of response for England as a whole, as well as for three regions that illustrate the main patterns of variation (the full data are set out in Part 2, Table 63). Across the country as a whole, three-fifths of respondents favoured region-alist solutions, with a third picking elected assemblies as the best solution and the remainder opting for regional bodies composed of appointed business people and local authority representatives. A quarter of respondents favoured government officials deciding, but only half of these espoused a clear preference for national ministers and departments to retain control. The range of support for elected assemblies ran from a quarter to two-fifths of respondents across regions, while that for appointed regional bodies stretched from under a sixth to nearly two-fifths. Between one in 16 and one in six respondents favoured continued central governance across different regions. These results seem consistent with earlier 1999 data which found support for regional assemblies varying between 37 and 51 per cent in England, with London at 60 per cent.[3] Answers to a general value question asking respondents to agree or disagree that government power in Britain is too centralised (see Table 9) similarly show a strengthening pattern of agreement over the period 1991–2000, especially notable after allowing for a slight change in the question options to allow a neutral response in 2000.

Table 9:   Is government power in Britain too centralised? (1991–2000)

A Strongly agree %
B Tend to agree %
C Neither agree nor disagree %
D Tend to disagree %
E Strongly disagree %
F Don't know %
G Net ' strongly agree' minus 'strongly disagree' %

	A	B	C	D	E	F	G
2000	29	31	16	9	4	10	+25
1991	17	43	—	16	2	2	+15

British Democracy

Finally, the 'State of the Nation' polls have tracked responses to questions on the state of democracy in the United Kingdom since two of us first devised the questions for Channel 4 in 1994. In 2000, respondents were asked to say how democratic Britain was 'in terms of what you consider to be important in a democracy'. Only 11 per cent said the country was 'very democratic', and most people (59 per cent) said 'fairly democratic'. This pattern of responses is almost identical with that in 1994 to the ICM survey for Channel 4, using the same question. Just over a fifth of people said Britain was 'not very democratic' or 'not at all democratic'. Asked in 2000, 'Do you think this country is getting more or less democratic?', over half (54 per cent) said 'less democratic' and only a fifth (22 per cent) said 'more demo-cratic', with the remainder 'don't knows'. In the run–up to the June election in 2001, opinion had switched and was more evenly divided, with 36 per cent each saying that the country was getting 'more' and 'less' democratic.

The public response to a parallel question illuminates one area where people feel that they possess rather 'less' democracy than they want. In 2000, some 70 per cent agreed that ordinary voters should have 'a great deal' or 'a fair amount' of power over government policies between elections, but only 19 per cent felt that they had such power; 44 per cent 'a little' power; and a third 'none at all'. This contradiction between the degree of power people wish to possess and the power they feel they possess in practice is broadly in line with previous questions on this theme in 1994 and 1996 (see Table 10), but there has been a marginal drop under the Labour government among those seeking a 'great deal' of power and a corresponding small rise in people satisfied with enjoying a 'little' or 'no' power. But the feeling of not possessing a 'great deal' or 'fair amount' of power is essentially unchanged.

Table 10: **How much power do people want between elections – and how much power do they believe they have? (1994, 1996 and 2000)**

| | 1994 | | 1996 | | 2000 | |
	Should	Do	Should	Do	Should	Do
A great deal	31	2	34	2	25	4
A fair amount	47	14	44	11	45	15
A little	12	53	15	50	17	44
None at all	4	26	4	35	8	32
Don't know	6	6	3	3	5	5

Conclusions

Taken overall, these results suggest considerable public support for deepening British democracy and a worrying level of public distrust in politicians and the political process. Public opinion seems at first to have been supportive of Labour's reform proposals and more confident about the way their country is governed; and after a dip in confidence, there were signs in 2000 and 2001 of a partial recovery in confidence in British democracy and governance. However, Labour's initial ambitions to transform Britain's 'over-centralised, secretive and discredited system of government' and to restore trust in politics have failed to win over the public. The new government began well after 1997 and constitutional reforms, especially the Human Rights Act and devolution, have been popular. The fact that people in Scotland, Wales and London broadly want

their new institutions to have more power is a general sign of their acceptance. But the passage of time and accumulation of avoidable problems in
Labour's governing style – centralist, elitist, manipulative and mildly sleazy
– have clearly been damaging in terms of public opinion. And the government's response to accusations of sleaze right up to the 2001 election – that
they will not respond since the public are interested only in 'the real issues'
– seems badly misplaced. While public opinion on freedom of information
is diffuse and not salient in terms of direct political pressure, the FOIA is not
likely to command great public confidence over time. A gulf seems to be
looming between the electorate's continued strong inclination towards
greater openness and reform, and the tendency of Labour ministers in
power to back-pedal on democratic and pluralist changes in favour of
keeping the levers of power in their own hands. The coming reform issue
after 2001 may well prove to be English regionalism, where there is wider
public backing for elected English assemblies than has been generally
realised, and signs of renewed interest in this issue among the higher
echelons of government. But electoral reform is likely to be a thorn in
Labour's side, divisive both internally and in its relations with the Liberal
Democrats nationally and in Scotland, and potentially damaging in terms of
public opinion. The promised review of the position after the Scottish and
Welsh elections could warm up the issue in advance of a commitment to a
referendum. We hope that the 'State of the Nation' polls will continue to
measure public opinion and strengthen the people's voices.

We fear that constitutional and governance issues and the sense of
promises unfulfilled charted here are likely to constitute only a subtext to
the politics of Labour's second term.

Notes

1   The poll was commissioned from ICM for the CHC Commission on the National Health Service, chaired by Will Hutton. The results are published in the commission report, *New Life for Health*, (Vintage, 2000)

2   See P. Dunleavy, H. Margetts and S. Weir, *Politico's Guide to Electoral Reform in Britain*, (Politico's, London, 1998), for a general guide to AV-Plus; and Dunleavy and Margetts, 'Mixed Electoral Systems and the Jenkins Commission on electoral reform in Britain', (*British Journal of Politics and International Relations*, 1991, vol. 1)

3   *The Economist*, (27 March 1999). See also R. Hazell, 'Shrinking Westminster', (*Guardian*, 3 January 2001).

Part two

Poll data, or what the people say

Part 2 summarises the results of the 'State of the Nation' polls and polls on specific issues sponsored by the Joseph Rowntree Reform Trust from 1991 to 2001, as well as the polls run in 1992, 1997 and 1998 to establish the likely results of the general elections in 1992 and 1997 under alternative electoral systems, including AV-Plus, and a special one-off poll in 1998 on the List PR system proposed for the Euro-elections. These electoral polls were sponsored by the JRRT, its sister trust, the Joseph Rowntree Charitable Trust, and the Economic and Social Research Council. Results from some other polls, including a poll by ICM Research for Channel 4, are included.

The figures given here record only total responses. Some of the questions have been simplified by removing preambles and other material. Almost none of the data here are broken down by gender, age, class, locality, party allegiance, voting intentions and similar data. Nor do we record the responses to every question asked, usually because they have become outdated by events. These additional data are available through the polling organisations. We list below details of the polls on which this report draws.

State of the Nation polls

State of the nation, 1991, MORI: summarises the key findings of a major study of public attitudes to, and participation in, the democratic process. MORI interviewed a total of 1,547 adults aged 18+ across 180 constituency sampling points throughout Great Britain. Interviews were conducted face to face, in homes, between 7 and 25 March 1991.

State of the Nation qualitative research, 1991, MORI: main findings from a series of six group discussions conducted on behalf of the Rowntree Reform Trust. MORI conducted six group discussions among members of the general public at three separate locations between 21 and 23 January 1991.

State of the Nation, 1995, MORI: report on first major follow-up poll from the 1991 survey. MORI interviewed a total of 2,141 adults aged 18+ in 313 enumeration district sampling points across Great Britain between 21 April and 8 May 1995.

State of the Nation, 1996, ICM Research: ICM Research interviewed a tightly controlled quota sample of 1,000 respondents between 10 September and 13 September 1996. Quotas were set of age, sex, class and working status. At the analysis stage, the results were weighted to the exact profile of all adults. Interviewing took place in respondents' homes.

State of the Nation, 2000, ICM: ICM interviewed a quota sample of 2,041 adults aged 18+ in the street between 23 and 28 October 2000. The sample was boosted in England, Wales and Scotland, and among ethnic minorities.

State of the Nation, 2001, ICM: ICM interviewed a random sample of 1,005 adults aged 18+ by telephone between 20 and 22 April 2001. Interviews were conducted across the country and the results were weighted to the profile of all adults.

Additional polls in the series

The Scott inquiry poll, February 1996, ICM: ICM interviewed 808 adults aged over 18 on 16, 17 and 19 February. Interviews were conducted across the country by phone and results weighted to be representative of all adults.

Poll on police powers, 1997, ICM: ICM interviewed a random sample of 1,201 adults aged 18+ by telephone between 3 and 5 January 1997. Interviews were conducted across the country and the results have been weighted to the profile of all adults.

Reform of the second chamber, 1999, ICM: ICM interviewed a random sample of 1,001 adults aged 18+ by telephone between 27 and 28 August 1999. Interviews were conducted across the country and the results have been weighted to the profile of all adults.

Democratising the National Health Service, 2000, ICM: ICM interviewed a random sample of 1,004 adults aged 18+ by telephone between 24 and 26 March 2000. Interviews were conducted across the country and the results have been weighted to the profile of all adults.

Other polls on democracy issues

Poll on democracy, 1994, ICM, for Channel 4: ICM interviewed a tightly controlled quota sample of 1,427 adults aged 18+ in 103 randomly selected constituencies countrywide. Interviews were conducted face to face in respondents' homes between 11 and 12 March 1994. The results were weighted to be representative of the adult population.

MORI poll on political attitudes, 1998, MORI, Conducted for *The Times*: MORI interviewed a representative quota sample of 1,926 adults aged 18+ at 164 sampling points across Great Britain in April–May 1998

Polls on the electoral process

Poll on electoral reform, 1977, Opinion Research Centre: this survey was carried out for the National Committee for Electoral Reform by the former polling organisation, ORC, who interviewed a nationwide quota sample of 1,410 electors aged 18 or over. Interviewing for the main component of the survey – a national cross-section of 1,176 electors – took place in 100 constituencies, and was supplemented by "booster" samples in Scotland and Wales to provide readable sub-samples. Fieldwork took place between 25 February and 2 March 1977.

Alternative ballots and electability, 1991, MORI: MORI interviewed a representative quota sample of 1,793 adults aged 18+ at 148 constituency sampling points across Great Britain. Interviews were conducted face to face, in homes on 23 to 27 August 1991.

The 1992 general election: how people would have voted under different electoral systems, ICM: ICM began polling respondents on the Friday after polling day (10 April) and largely completed polling by Tuesday 14 April. Interviewing continued for two more days in Scotland because of the large boosted sample there. The total sample achieved over the ten standard regions in England and Wales and three regions in Scotland was 9,694 interviews. Details of the weighting and other technical information can be found in P. Dunleavy, H. Margetts and S. Weir, *Replaying the 1992 General Election*, (LSE Public Policy Group, 1992)

Remodelling the 1997 general election, full Interview Survey – vols 1 and 2,

Combined Survey – vols 1 and 2, ICM: reports on two independent surveys designed to provide authoritative and impartial information on how the British electorate would have voted under alternative electoral systems at the time of the 1997 general election. The study was split into two independent surveys, one of which was designed to provide a sufficiently robust sample making extensive data interrogation possible; while the other, smaller survey included additional questions on attitudes towards both the concept of proportional representation and towards the political parties. A total of 8,447 interviews were conducted for the re-modelling exercise between 2 and 6 May, 1997. Interviews were conducted face to face, in street. A total of 1,901 interviews were conducted for the attitudes study between 2 and 6 May, 1997. Interviews were conducted face to face, in the street. Research funded by the ESRC and Rowntree Charitable Trust.

Open or closed list voting for the European Parliament election, 1998, ICM: ICM interviewed a quota sample of 1,330 adults aged 18+ nationwide in early February 1998.

PR poll, 1998, ICM: ICM interviewed a quota sample of 1,612 adults aged 18+ in the street, February 1998. The findings were then weighted for representativeness. This poll was undertaken to calculate the results of AV-Plus elections.

Reports on electoral studies

Replaying the 1992 general election: how Britain would have voted under alternative electoral systems, Patrick Dunleavy, Helen Margetts and Stuart Weir (LSE Public Policy Paper No. 3, London School of Economics, 1992)

Making votes count: replaying the 1990s general elections under alternative electoral systems, Patrick Dunleavy, Helen Margetts, Brendan O'Duffy and Stuart Weir (Democratic Audit Paper No. 11 in association with the LSE Public Policy Group and Birkbeck College, London, Human Rights Centre, University of Essex, 1997)

Devolution votes: PR elections in Scotland and Wales, Patrick Dunleavy, Helen Margetts and Stuart Weir (Democratic Audit Paper No. 11, Human Rights Centre, University of Essex, 1997)

Making votes count 2: special report on mixed voting systems, Patrick Dunleavy, Helen Margetts and Stuart Weir, Democratic Audit Paper No. 14, (in association with the LSE Public Policy Group and Birkbeck College, London), Human Rights Centre, University of Essex 1998

Politico's guide to electoral reform in Britain: Patrick Dunleavy, Helen Margetts and Stuart Weir, (Politico's 1998)

The poll data

Labour's constitutional agenda (1997)

People interviewed in 1996 gave strong backing to New Labour's constitutional agenda in 1997, with consensus levels of support for a Bill of Rights and a Freedom of Information Act (along with control of inflation). However, support for devolution throughout the UK was lukewarm, with a 40:33 per cent majority for a Scottish parliament and only 36:34 per cent for a Welsh assembly. In general, there was ambivalence or genuine confusion about the devolution question. A large minority of 30 per cent were 'don't knows' on the

Voices of the people

Welsh question, 27 per cent on Scottish devolution, and 22 per cent on English regional assemblies.

Table 1: Labour's constitutional proposals (ICM 1996)

If Labour wins the next general election they have promised to do the following. For each please say whether you approve or disapprove

Set up a Scottish parliament with devolved powers

	%
Approve	40
Disapprove	33
Don't know	27

Set up a Welsh assembly with devolved powers

	%
Approve	36
Disapprove	34
Don't know	30

Hold a referendum to give the public the opportunity to choose a new voting system

	%
Approve	65
Disapprove	20
Don't know	15

Pass a Freedom of Information Act giving ordinary people a right of access to government information

	%
Approve	73
Disapprove	15
Don't know	12

Abolish the right of hereditary peers to be in the House of Lords

	%
Approve	57
Disapprove	25
Don't know	18

Introduce a Bill of Rights to protect individual liberties

	%
Approve	81
Disapprove	7
Don't know	12

Give people in all areas of England the opportunity to choose whether or not to have a regional assembly

	%
Approve	63
Disapprove	15
Don't know	22

Voices of the people

Give top priority to keeping inflation down

	%
Approve	79
Disapprove	11
Don't know	10

UK democracy

Most people place Britain in the middle of the democratic spectrum. Broadly, three times as many people think Britain is very or fairly democratic as not very or not at all democratic. In detail, 59 per cent thought Britain was 'fairly democratic' in 2000 and 11 per cent 'very democratic'; 16 per cent thought it was 'not very democratic', and only 6 per cent that it was 'not at all democratic'. The distribution of opinions remained fairly constant between 1994 and 2000.

However, over a third of people believe that Britain is becoming 'less' democratic. The proportion of those agreeing that the UK has become 'less democratic' rose by 15 per cent between 1994 and 2000 (from 39 to 54 per cent). As the 2000 poll did not offer the 'no change' option given in the 1994 poll, however, this may have contributed to a disproportionate increase. By April 2001, dissatisfaction was falling and the population became evenly divided, at 36 per cent each thinking the country has become 'less' or 'more' democratic.

Most respondents had a rights-based conception of the nature of democracy. In 2000, 65 and 42 per cent of people agreed that 'living in a free country' and 'an equal society' were democracy's most important aspects. By comparison, just 10 per cent (13 in 1994) suggested that a free market economy was its most crucial element.

People want more power between elections, but do not believe that they possess that power.

Table 2:   How democratic is Britain? Are we more or less democratic? (ICM poll for Channel 4, 1994)

In terms of what you consider to be important in a democracy, do you think Britain is…?

	1994	1996	2000
Very democratic	14	11	11
Fairly democratic	59	53	59
Not very democratic	17	20	16
Not at all democratic	4	7	6
Don't know	6	9	8

Do you think this country is getting more or less democratic?

	1994	2000	2001
More democratic	12	22	36
Less democratic	39	54	36
No change	42	–	16
Don't know	7	24	12

Voices of the people

Table 3: Democratic values (MORI 1995)

Which two of the things that people say are important about democracy do you think are most important about democracy?

	1994	1995
Living in a free country	64	65
An equal society	38	42
Voting for a government in elections	31	27
Strong and effective government	27	27
Popular control over government decisions	17	22
A free market economy	13	10
Other	2	1
None of these	4	4
Don't know	4	2

Table 4: How much power do people want between elections – and how much power do they believe they have? (ICM 1996, 2000 and 2001)

	1994		1996		2000	
	Should	Do	Should	Do	Should	Do
A great deal	31	2	34	2	25	4
A fair amount	47	14	44	11	45	15
A little	12	53	15	50	17	44
None at all	4	26	4	35	8	32
Don't know	6	6	3	3	5	5

The governing system

Faith in the existing system of government is generally low. From 1973, the proportion of people saying that 'the present system of governing Britain' could be 'improved quite a lot' or 'needs a great deal of improvement' rose from just under half in 1973 to peaks of 69, 73 and 72 per cent in the mid-1990s. Opinion has see-sawed under the Labour government.. In 1998, the figure for respondents looking for improvement fell to 54 per cent, rose again to nearly two-thirds of respondents in 2000, and fell again – in the midst of the foot-and-mouth epidemic – to 56 per cent in 2001. Still not good. Sixty per cent of respondents have consistently agreed that British government is 'too centralised'; and in the 1990s, people tended to think that British government was out of date and needed to be reformed on 'more European lines'. There has been constant support for a written constitution providing 'clear legal rules' for ministers and civil servants; and people in the 1990s also rated constitutional checks and balances on government higher than freedom of decisive action for government. Finally, the NHS is outstandingly the most important institution so far as the public is concerned; parliament comes a poor second.

Table 5:   Faith in the governing system

Which of these statements best describes your opinion on the present system of governing Britain?

	1973	1977	1991	1994	1995	1996	1998	2000	2001
Works extremely well and could not be improved	5	10	4	2	3	1	4	1	3
Could be improved in small ways but mainly works well	43	24	29	26	19	25	37	30	39
Could be improved quite a lot	35	33	40	39	40	44	39	40	31

cont'd . . .

Voices of the people

	1973	1977	1991	1994	1995	1996	1998	2000	2001
Needs a great deal of improvement	14	29	23	30	35	28	15	24	25
Don't know	4	4	5	4	3	2	5	5	2

Table 6: British government is out of date

Agreement with the proposal that the system of government in Britain is out of date

	1991	1995
Strongly agree	16	18
Tend to agree	29	32
Neither agree nor disagree	16	17
Tend to disagree	26	22
Strongly disagree	8	6
Don't know	5	5

Table 7: Britain needs a more European style of government

Agreement with the statement Britain needs to modernise its political system so as to operate on more European lines

	1992
Agree strongly	30
Agree slightly	23
Neither agree nor disagree	11
Disagree slightly	11
Disagree strongly	17
Don't know/not sure	9

Table 8:   British government is too centralised

Agreement with the proposal that government power in Britain is too centralised

	1991	1994	2000
Strongly agree	17	21	29
Tend to agree	43	41	31
Neither agree nor disagree	17	16	16
Tend to disagree	16	13	9
Strongly disagree	2	2	4
Don't know	5	8	10

Table 9:   Strong versus consensual government

A *It is important for a government to be strong and stable, even if it occasionally goes too far*

B *Achieving agreement is important for a government, even if it means more elections*

	A Strongly agree/ Prefer	Neutral	B Strongly agree/ Prefer	Neutral
1991	43	14	38	4
1995	38	14	43	5

Table 10:   Constitutional checks and balances

A *It is important for a government to be able to take decisive action without looking over its shoulder all the time*

B *Constitutional checks and balances are important to make sure that a government doesn't overdo it*

	A Strongly agree/ Prefer	Neutral	B Strongly agree/ Prefer	Neutral
1991	32	16	47	4
1995	27	15	53	5

Voices of the people

Table 11: Written constitution

Britain needs a written constitution, providing clear legal rules within which government ministers and civil servants are forced to operate

	1995	1996	2000
Strongly agree	37	30	38
Tend to agree	42	44	33
Neither agree nor disagree	9	9	14
Tend to disagree	5	7	3
Strongly disagree	1	2	2
Don't know/no opinion	6	8	10

Table 12: Important institutions in Britain

Which of the following institutions in this country is the most valuable institution for this country?

	2000
The BBC	4
The Benefits Agency	2
The National Health Service	63
The police	11
The Bank of England	2
The Royal Family	3
Parliament	12
Don't know/not sure	4

And which would you put second?

	2000
The BBC	7
The Benefits Agency	8
The National Health Service	17

cont'd . . .

	2000
The police	44
The Bank of England	5
The Royal Family	4
Parliament	14
Don't know/not sure	–

Sources: Crowther-Hunt 1973; ORC 1977; MORI 1991, 1995 and (MORI Poll for The Times) 1998; ICM 1994, 1996 and 2000; ICM poll on the NHS 2000

The powers and role of the monarchy

In 1996, the public remained generally in favour of the Queen's constitutional and political role in dissolving Parliament, choosing a Prime Minister, addressing the nation on Christmas Day and outlining government policy at the beginning of Parliament. However, there is a two-to-one majority for reorganising the monarchy along more modest continental lines. There is a majority (40:33 per cent) for removing the Church of England's status as the established religion.

Table 13: A more continental monarchy?

Agreement with the view that the monarchy in Britain should be reorganised on more modest continental lines

	1996
Agree strongly	21
Agree	31
Neither agree nor disagree	16
Disagree	18
Disagree strongly	9
Don't know	4

Voices of the people

Table 14: The Queen's constitutional roles (1996)

The Queen performs the following constitutional and political roles. Please could you tell me if you think the Queen should retain them or not?

Dissolving Parliament and calling an election

	%
Retain the power	58
Lose the power	31
Don't know	11

Choosing who to appoint as Prime Minister

	%
Retain the power	46
Lose the power	42
Don't know	12

Addressing the nation on Christmas Day

	%
Retain the power	69
Lose the power	22
Don't know	8

Outlining the policy of the government in the Queen's Speech at the opening of Parliament

	%
Retain the power	62
Lose the power	28
Don't know	10

Table 15: The status of the Church of England

Agreement with the view that the Church of England should not remain the official religion of the country headed by the monarchy

	1996
Agree strongly	15
Agree	25
Neither agree nor disagree	20
Disagree	21
Disagree strongly	12
Don't know	7

Source: ICM 1996

The role of Parliament

More than half the population take the view that Parliament doesn't have sufficient control over the executive; in 2000, four times as many people took this view as felt that Parliament had enough control. In the 1990s, people tended to think that Parliament worked 'very' or 'fairly' well, though satisfaction fell from 59 per cent in 1991 to just 43 per cent in 1995; dissatisfaction rose over the same period from 16 to 30 per cent. Broadly speaking,

half or more of the electorate think that the terms of Parliament should be
fixed to remove the Prime Minister's power to decide election dates, and
about a quarter disagree, another quarter or so are unmoved or undecided.
In 2000, support for a fixed-term Parliament rose to a high point of 60 per
cent.

Table 16:   Parliamentary control of the executive

Agreement with the statement that parliament does not have sufficient control over what the government does

	1977	**1991**	**1994**	**1995**	**2000**
Strongly agree	12	10	32	13	21
Tend to agree	31	40	32	39	32
Neither agree nor disagree	25	19	–	21	20
Tend to disagree	–	20	16	15	8
Strongly disagree	12	3	7	3	4
Don't know	20	9	12	9	15

Table 17:   Parliamentary performance

Overall, how well or badly do you think Parliament works?

	1991	**1995**
Very well	5	4
Fairly well	54	39
Neither well nor badly	21	22
Fairly badly	12	19
Very badly	4	11
Don't know	4	6

Table 18 : Fixed-term Parliaments

Agreement with the statement that the length of Parliament should be fixed, removing the Prime Minister's power to choose the date of the next election

	1991	1995	2000	2001
Strongly agree	21	23	31	24
Tend to agree	35	34	29	26
Neither agree nor disagree	16	18	17	17
Tend to disagree	18	12	7	14
Strongly disagree	5	6	6	11
Don't know	5	6	10	8

Sources: ORC 1977; MORI 1991; ICM Channel 4, 1994; MORI 1995; ICM 2000 and 2001.

Reform of the House of Lords

Most people want to see the House of Lords replaced and modernised, and there is strong, but not decisive, support for an elected second chamber. A significant minority in 1995 wanted to abolish the House of Lords and the idea of a second chamber altogether, while just under a third of respondents in 1991 and 1996 were opposed to any change at all. The crucial political issue now is between a largely elected and largely appointed second chamber. In 1999, 61 per cent wanted to see all members elected, and only a third a partly elected, partly appointed chamber; by 2000, broadly 60 per cent wanted either a wholly elected second chamber, or one with a majority of elected over appointed members, rather than the government's strong preference for a largely appointed chamber, as recommended by the Royal Commission on the Future of the House of Lords.

People generally back the idea of a second chamber with real powers to block legislation that members are not satisfied with – even to the point of giving peers the powers of indefinite delay where issues are not resolved – and believe that an elected chamber can do so with more legitimacy than an appointed chamber. There was particular support for giving the second chamber extra powers to delay laws that might endanger human rights. However, the 2000 poll picked up signs of fatigue on the part of the public, with about a quarter of 'don't knows' both on the composition of the second chamber and its powers.

Table 19: Support for an elected second chamber

Support for replacing the House of Lords with an elected second chamber

	1991
Strongly support	17
Tend to support	23
Neither/nor	23
Tend to oppose	19
Strongly oppose	10
Don't know	8

Table 20: Reform options for the House of Lords

The future of the House of Lords is being discussed. Which of these proposals, if any, do you think is the best course?

	1991	
Leave it as it is	27	
Remove hereditary peers' right to speak and vote	15	
Replace the House of Lords with an elected second chamber	25	*cont'd . . .*

	1991
Abolish the House of Lords and have no second chamber	15
Other/none of these	2
Don't know	17

Table 21: Who should make law in the new second chamber?

When it comes to making new laws in the new second chamber, whose views do you think should be considered more important?

The views of eminent people who have special knowledge or expertise			The views of elected representatives of ordinary people
much more important	12	34	much more important
a little more important	14	26	a little more important
ns	2	4	ns
Don't know		8	Don't know

The column totals are 28 and 64.

Table 22: An elected or partly elected, partly appointed second chamber?

There are two ways in which the government might seek to draw on people with special knowledge or expertise for the second chamber. Which do you think is preferable?

	1999
All members elected	61
Partly elected/partly appointed	33
Don't know	5

79

Voices of the people

Out of the following situations, which do you think would give the reformed House of Lords most right to block government legislation?

	2000
If the reformed House of Lords were wholly elected	26
If it were mostly elected, with a minority of appointed members	33
If it were mostly appointed, with a minority of elected members	14
Don't know	27

Table 23: Blocking powers of the second chamber

In helping to make and improve new laws, what powers do you think the second chamber should have to make the government think again when it objects to a new law?

	1999	2000
The power to delay a new law for a few months	21	22
The power to delay a new law for one year	19	20
The power to delay a new law for two years	6	6
The power to hold up a new law indefinitely until the two Houses of Parliament can reach agreement	46	31
Don't know	8	21

Table 24: Protecting human rights in the second chamber

Agreement with the view that the new second chamber should have extra powers of delay where it feels that a proposed law would endanger human rights

	1999
Agree	72
Disagree	20
Don't know/not sure	8

Source: ICM 1999 and 2000.

The role and duties of MPs

Most people agree that representing and being loyal to constituency interests is the most important duty of MPs, and very few believe that their prime loyalty should be to the views of their party, party conference or party leader.

Table 25: Who should MPs be loyal to?

In your opinion, do you think MPs should be most loyal to . . .

	1996
The interests of their constituents	65
The views of their local party	12
The national party leader	4
The views of their party conference	2
Their own conscience	11
Don't know	5

Table 26: The duties of MPs

MPs have various duties. Which of these is the most important?

	1996
Supporting their party loyally in votes in Parliament	8
Representing constituency interests	39
Taking up individual constituents' problems and grievances	17
Ensuring that government does its job efficiently and honestly	31
Voting and acting in line with their own judgement	4
Don't know	2

And which is the second most important?

	1996
Supporting their party loyally in votes in Parliament	8
Representing constituency interests	27
Taking up individual constituents' problems and grievances	27
Ensuring that government does its job efficiently and honestly	30
Voting and acting in line with their own judgement	7
Don't know	1

Policing the conduct and interests of ministers and MPs

There are growing and high levels of support for more independent scrutiny of government ministers' conduct. In 2000, only 7 per cent supported the present way of disciplining ministers through the Prime Minister (4 per cent less than in 1995), leaving a total of 70 per cent who wanted accusations of serious professional misconduct to be investigated by an independent

222

222

2222

2222

22222

commission or the police (78 per cent in 1995). In general the public accepted in the 1990s that MPs may carry on with a trade or profession while being an MP, but there was evident concern about abuse of their position for financial gain and rising support for a ban on activities which may financially benefit MPs. Two thirds of respondents were in favour of stronger independent scrutiny and governance of MPs' conduct in 1995, although this had fallen by 5 per cent in 2000. Only 7 per cent supported the existing system of scrutinising MPs' conduct in the 2000 poll.

Table 27: The legitimacy of MPs' interests

I am going to read out a list of things that some MPs do. Which, if any, do you think they should be allowed to do?

	1995	1996
Having any paid job outside Parliament	28	28
Being paid to write articles for newspapers and magazines	35	–
Receiving fees from private companies in return for lobbying on their behalf at Westminster	3	8
Being sponsored by trade unions towards election and campaigning costs in their constituencies	21	24
Carrying on a trade or profession (eg. as a farmer, lawyer, dentist, etc.) while being an MP	45	–
Being the paid representative of a non-commercial interest group (eg., the Police Federation)	21	17
Keeping secret some of the payments made to them by companies or interest groups on the grounds that these payments have nothing to do with their parliamentary duties	–	8

cont'd . . .

Voices of the people

	1995	1996
Receiving fees from specialist lobbying companies to promote their clients' interests at Westminster	2	–
Asking questions in Parliament for money	3	–
Speaking or voting on issues where they stand to gain financially	4	7
Speaking or voting on issues which affect commercial interests or private companies from which they receive payments	4	–
Deciding in the House of Commons how much MPs should get paid	–	15
Other	1	–
Don't know	8	–
None of these	22	–

Table 28: Prohibitions on MPs' activities

And which, if any, do you think MPs should be banned from doing?

	1995	1996
Having any paid job outside Parliament	48	61
Being paid to write articles for newspapers and magazines	43	–
Receiving fees from private companies in return for lobbying on their behalf at Westminster	78	87
Being sponsored by trade unions towards election and campaigning costs in their constituencies	48	62
Carrying on a trade or profession (eg. as a farmer, lawyer, dentist, etc.) while being an MP	33	–

cont'd . . .

	1995	1996
Being the paid representative of a non-commercial interest group (eg., the Police Federation)	44	70
Keeping secret some of the payments made to them by companies or interest groups on the grounds that these payments have nothing to do with their parliamentary duties	–	86
Receiving fees from specialist lobbying companies to promote their clients' interests at Westminster	76	–
Asking questions in Parliament for money	83	–
Speaking or voting on issues where they stand to gain financially	77	86
Speaking or voting on issues which affect commercial interests or private companies from which they receive payments	73	–
Deciding in the House of Commons how much MPs should get paid	–	74
Other	1	–
Don't know	3	–
None of these	1	–

Voices of the people

Table 29: Making and enforcing the MPs' rule book

I'd like you to think now about how Parliament is run. At the moment, MPs as a whole make and enforce the rules that govern their conduct in Parliament. (Sentence added in 2000: They are advised by a Commissioner for Standards who investigates complaints against individual MPs.) Which of these comes closest to your own view about these rules?

	1995	2000
The existing system of rules, with MPs making and enforcing them, works well and should not be changed	8	7
The existing rules should be tightened up and enforced by MPs, without involving the police, courts or any outside body	19	21
The rules should be made law, with an independent commission and civil courts overseeing the MPs' conduct	38	34
The rules should be made law, making breaches a crime investigated by the police and punishable by the criminal courts	29	29
Don't know	7	10

Table 30: Responsibility for the conduct of ministers

How do you think accusations of serious professional misconduct by government ministers should be investigated?

	1995	2000
The Prime Minister should make enquiries, as now, into whether allegations are true and decide if the minister should resign	11	7
The House of Commons should make enquiries and decide if the minister should resign	12	16
An independent official commission should investigate and decide whether ministers should resign	47	42

cont'd . . .

	1995	2000
The police should investigate and decide whether or not ministers should face legal trial in court	29	28
Don't know	3	8

Table 31: Ex-ministers' job opportunities

Do you think MPs should or should not be allowed to take jobs in companies they have dealt with as government ministers within two years of leaving office?

	1995
Should	15
Should not	78
Don't know	8

Source: MORI 1995; ICM 1996 and 2000

Perceptions of sleaze under the Blair government

Sleaze in government was widely perceived to be a significant problem in Britain in 2000. The most significant issues were untruthful government ministers and financial sleaze, with some nine out of ten people seeing these as problems, major or minor. Close behind came patronage, cronyism and spin-doctoring the media. Only between 4 and 8 per cent of respondents did not regard the various manifestations of sleaze as a problem at all.

Voices of the people

Table 32: What kinds of sleaze are a problem in Britain today? (2000)

Financial sleaze

	%
A major problem	49
A minor problem	39
Not a problem at all	6
Don't know	6

Ministers appointing friends to important public posts

	%
A major problem	50
A minor problem	36
Not a problem at all	7
Don't know	7

Using spin-doctors to manipulate the media

	%
A major problem	57
A minor problem	30
Not a problem at all	5
Don't know	8

Appointing large party donors to government committees and task forces

	%
A major problem	52
A minor problem	35
Not a problem at all	6
Don't know	8

Granting peerages and honours to people who have made large financial donations to political parties

	%
A major problem	52
A minor problem	32
Not a problem at all	8
Don't know	8

Government ministers favouring major private interests before the interests of ordinary people

	%
A major problem	58
A minor problem	29
Not a problem at all	6
Don't know	6

Voices of the people

Government ministers not being truthful?

	%
A major problem	66
A minor problem	26
Not a problem at all	4
Don't know	5

Source: ICM 2000

Trust in government and politics

Table 33: Trust in government advice

Do you trust government ministers and their advisory committees to tell you the truth about . . .

The safety of food we eat

	1996	2000
Yes	16	20
No	78	74
Don't know	6	6

The safety of nuclear installations

	1996	2000
Yes	16	18
No	78	75
Don't know	6	7

Safe sex and AIDS

	1996	2000
Yes	41	43
No	47	47
Don't know	12	9

The safety of British beef

	1996	2000
Yes	19	27
No	73	67
Don't know	8	7

The safety of medicines

	1996	2000
Yes	32	37
No	60	55
Don't know	9	8

The safety of GM foods and crops

	2000
Yes	20
No	74
Don't know	6

Table 34: Choice between government and independent advice

Who should advise the public about scientific health and safety issues?

	2000
Ministers and civil servants within government departments	7
An advisory committee of experts appointed by and responsible to ministers	25
An independent committee of experts	66
Don't know	3

Source: ICM 1996 and 2000

Electoral reform

Since 1992, the public has generally in principle backed the proposal that general elections in Britain should be proportional, with between 54 and 60 per cent backing PR, and between 15 and 27 per cent against. In 2000, support for proportionality stood at 60 per cent, with half of these expressing 'strong' support. Further, ICM has three times put a mock referendum question to respondents, in 1997, 1998 and 2000. Opinion swung gradually further towards a PR alternative to the existing system. In 1997, opinion was marginally in favour of the additional-member PR system (AMS) over the existing first-past-the-post system; by 2000, people expressed a clear preference for AMS. Further, in 2000 people voted heavily for a referendum, on PR by 56 per cent to only 15 per cent against.

However, as Part 1 notes and several tables below demonstrate, people's responses do vary with the tenor of the questions put to them, and opinions about the existing electoral system in Britain vary according to the angle of the question. Thus, there is substantial support (though not an overall majority) for the statement that we should keep the existing system as it is more likely to produce 'single-party government' or when presented as a means of ensuring strong and effective government (31 per cent in 2000). However, other responses suggest that the British public may be willing to accept the idea of alternative voting systems, if they could be shown to remedy specific problems.

Table 35: Proportional representation

Agreement with the statement that this country should adopt a new voting system that would give parties seats in parliament in proportion to their share of votes

	1932	**1995**	**1995**	**1996**	**2000**
Strongly agree	38	16	24	37	31
Tend to agree	19	38	36	19	29
Neither agree nor disagree	10	14	13	14	14
Tend to disagree	9	13	13	9	7
Strongly disagree	18	6	4	16	8
Don't know	7	14	9	5	11

Voices of the people

Table 36: Mock referendum on electoral reform

Respondents were given a showcard with the pros and cons of both first-past-the-post and the additional-member system (see showcard, page 28). The interviewer explained that the card showed the choice people may get in a government referendum on the voting system for elections for MPs to go to the House of Commons, and were asked to look at the card carefully and to vote for one or the other alternative

	1997*	1998**	2000
The existing system of voting	41	36	27
A proportional system of voting	45	40	53
Don't know	14	24	20

* The question in the 1997 poll read: 'Which of the following systems would you choose?'
** The question in the 1998 poll read: 'Which of these two alternative electoral systems would you choose?'

Table 37: Public referendums on electoral reform

Agreement with the statement that a referendum should be held on changing the system we use to elect MPs

	1991	1995	2000
Strongly agree	43	46	27
Tend to agree	–	–	29
Neither agree nor disagree	–	–	18
Tend to disagree	–	–	8
Strongly disagree	44	43	7
Don't know	13	11	12

* The question in the State of the Nation 1991 and 1995 polls read: 'More specifically, would you personally like to see a referendum held to decide on each of the following?: Hold a referendum on changing the system we use to elect MPs'. The options for the 1991 poll were: Yes, hold/No, do not hold; options for the 1995 poll were: Yes, hold/No, do not hold/Don't know.

Table 38: Views on the current voting system

A Strongly agree

B Tend to agree

C Neither agree nor disagree

D Tend to disagree

E Strongly disagree

F Don't know

We should retain the current voting system as it is more likely to produce single-party government

	A	B	C	D	E	F
1992	28	15	10	15	24	8
1995	14	33	16	24	8	5
1997	29	12	17	16	20	5

The present system of voting is the only way the country can get strong one-party governments that will get things done

	A	B	C	D	E	F
1997	10	22	13	26	14	15
2000	31	29	14	7	8	11

The voting system produces governments which do not represent the views of most ordinary people

	A	B	C	D	E	F
1977★	24	38	—	16	8	14
1994	44	27	—	15	7	7
2000	26	30	18	12	5	9

★ In 1977 the options were 'a great deal'; 'quite a lot'; 'not very much'; and 'not at all'.

Voices of the people

Table 39: Public responses to various views on electoral systems

A *Strongly agree*
B *Tend to agree*
C *Neither agree nor disagree*
D *Tend to disagree*
E *Strongly disagree*
F *Don't know*

	A	B	C	D	E	F
It is much more important to have a voting system that works than one which is completely fair (1977)	19	29	15	22	9	6
Whatever kind of voting system we have, it won't make any difference to the problems we face in Britain (1977)	28	38	9	16	6	3
Whatever kind of voting system we have, it won't make any difference to the problems we face in Britain (1992)	28	19	11	14	21	6

Table 40: First-past-the-post and unrepresentative government

Agreement with the statement that the voting system produces governments which do not represent the views of most ordinary people

	1977*	1994	2000
Strongly agree	21	44	26
Tend to agree	34	27	30
Neither agree nor disagree	–	–	18
Tend to disagree	22	15	12
Strongly disagree	10	7	5
Don't know	13	7	9

★ The ORC 1977 opinion poll question read: 'How much, if at all, do you think each of the following are to blame for Britain's problems?: The voting system producing governments which do not represent the views of the public'. The response was graded: A great deal/Quite a lot/Not very much/Not at all/Don't know. The ICM 1994 opinion poll's response was graded: Agree a lot/Agree a little/Disagree a lot/Don't know.

Table 41: First-past-the-post and single-party government

Agreement with the statement that we should retain the current voting system as it is more likely to produce single-party government

	1992	1995	1997
Strongly agree	28	14	29
Tend to agree	15	33	12
Neither agree nor disagree	10	16	17
Tend to disagree	15	24	16
Strongly disagree	24	8	20
Don't know/no opinion	8	5	5

Table 42: Proportional representation in local elections

Agreement with the statement that elections for local authorities should use a voting system that would give parties seats on local councils in proportion to their share of the vote

	2000
Strongly agree	30
Tend to agree	31
Neither agree nor disagree	17
Tend to disagree	5
Strongly disagree	5
Don't know	12

Voices of the people

Table 43: Options under different electoral systems

A *Clearer differences between parties?*

B *More agreement and working together between parties*

	A Strongly agree/ Prefer	Neutral	B Strongly agree/ Prefer	Neutral
1991	23	16	57	3
1995	24	15	56	5

A *One MP to represent the area you live in*

B *Several MPs to represent a larger area, possibly from different parties*

	A Strongly agree/ Prefer	Neutral	B Strongly agree/ Prefer	Neutral
1991	51	13	32	4
1995	47	13	36	5
1997	83	—	9	7

A *Marking your ballot against one name, as present*

B *Marking your ballot so you could indicate your first, second and third choices*

	A Strongly agree/ Prefer	Neutral	B Strongly agree/ Prefer	Neutral
1991	48	10	37	4
1995	43	10	42	5

A   *One party in government with all others in opposition*

B   *Two or more parties forming a coalition government*

| | A | | B | |
	Strongly agree/ Prefer	Neutral	Strongly agree/ Prefer	Neutral
1991	45	17	35	4
1995	40	16	37	6

A   *The current electoral system should be retained as it preserves two strong parties, each able to form government*

B   *The two-party system is now an obstacle to progress in Britain by blocking the advance of other parties and narrowing the range of alternative policies*

| | A | | B | |
	Strongly agree/ Prefer	Neutral	Strongly agree/ Prefer	Neutral
1991	36	20	38	6
1995	36	22	37	6

Source: MORI 1991 and 1995; ICM 1997?

Referendums, election mandates and electoral power

A small majority of respondents in 2000 agreed that general election results should set government policy between elections, while in the 1990s varying majorities thought that voting alone did not give people enough power. One sign of the popular desire for greater participation in decision-making is the strong level of backing for referendums over a parliamentary monopoly of legislation and decision-making on important issues; and for a constitutional innovation to allow the public to petition for a referendum

Voices of the people

on a particular issue. All round, more than three-quarters of the population back the use of referendums in general and the idea of a petition. Polls in 1991 and 2000 show a shift in attitudes towards compulsory voting, moving from a smallish majority for compulsory voting in 1991, with 49 per cent in favour and 42 per cent against, to only 30 per cent in favour and a 49 per cent disapproval rate in 2000.

Table 44: Electoral mandates

Do you agree or disagree that general election results should set government policy until the next election?

	2000
Strongly agree	25
Tend to agree	28
Neither agree nor disagree	16
Tend to disagree	14
Strongly disagree	9
Don't know	9

Table 45: Electoral power over government

Do you think that voting every 4-5 years in a general election gives ordinary voters sufficient power over the way governments act or not?

	1994
Yes	33
No	60
Don't know	7

Agreement with the statement that holding general elections every 4-5 years does not give the public enough power over the way government acts

	1995
Strongly agree	19
Tend to agree	33
Neither agree nor disagree	14
Tend to disagree	23
Strongly disagree	6
Don't know	5

Table 46: Parliament and referendums

Should Parliament decide all important issues, or would you like Britain to adopt a referendum system whereby certain issues are put to the people to decide by popular vote?

	1991	1995
Parliament decides★	20	19
Referendum	75	77
Don't know	5	5

★   The question in the 1995 poll read 'Government decides' rather than 'Parliament decides'

Table 47: Petitioning for a referendum

In principle, do you think it would be a good or a bad idea if the British people could force the government to hold a referendum on a particular issue by raising a petition with signatures from, say, a million people?

	1991	1995
Bad idea	16	15
Good idea	77	77
Neither/no opinion	7	7

Voices of the people

Table 48: Compulsory voting

Agreement with the proposal that compulsory voting should be introduced in Britain, and people who do not vote at general elections might be fined

	1991*	2000
Strongly agree	27	14
Tend to agree	22	16
Neither agree nor disagree	9	14
Tend to disagree	21	15
Strongly disagree	21	34
Don't know	–	7

★   The wording in the 1991 poll was 'support', not 'agree'

Source: MORI 1991 and 1995; ICM 2000

Funding of political parties and election campaigns

The public have long wanted controls over election expenditure by political parties, as the 1991 poll suggests, but they were opposed to state funding for the election campaigns of political parties and were then also not keen on trade union or corporate contributions to the parties.

Table 49: State funding for parties' election campaigns

It has been suggested that during general elections a fixed amount of public money should be given to political parties to finance election campaigns. Do you think this a good idea or a bad idea?

	1991
Good idea	39
Bad idea	53
Don't know	8

Table 50: Trade union and corporate funding

Do you think contributions from trade unions should be banned, or not?

	%
Banned	46
Not banned	43
Don't know	11

And should contributions from companies be banned, or not?

	%
Banned	44
Not banned	45
Don't know	11

Table 51: Limits on election spending

Should there be or not be a set limit to the amount of money political parties can spend across the nation on general election campaigns?

	1991
Should	81
Should not	14
Don't know	5

Voices of the people

And should there be or should not be a set limit to the amount of money political parties can spend on local campaigning during general elections?

	1991
Should	80
Should not	14
Don't know	6

Source: MORI 1991

Coalitions

Respondents generally felt that coalition governments may produce more moderate government (49 per cent), more considered legislation (48 per cent), and government listening to more voters (46 per cent); on the other hand, they felt more strongly that coalitions result in weak and ineffective governments (60 per cent), uncertainty in financial markets (69 per cent) and more frequent elections (79 per cent). Thus perception of the weaknesses of coalition government was greater than that of its benefits. There has been increased dissatisfaction with single-party governments, however. In 1991, 49 per cent of interviewees agreed that one party should gain an overall majority and form a government. By 1998, agreement that the largest party should always form a government on its own had fallen to 36 per cent. Explicit support for non-majority governments increased by 1998: 43 per cent of respondents expressed a liking for a coalition government of two or more parties, while 37 per cent liked governments formed by a party with great support but no majority, or a coalition of parties with majority support.

Table 52: Single-party, minority and coalition government

Which of the options on this card comes closest to your own views on how the country should be run after the next election?

	1991
One party should gain an overall majority and form the government	49
No clear majority, but some parties should form a coalition government	23
No clear majority, but the largest party should form the government and seek co-operation of other parties on policies they can support	22
None of these	1
Don't know	5

Table 53: Public perceptions of a 'hung' Parliament before the 1997 election

If no party wins an overall majority of seats at the next general election, there could be a 'hung parliament'. In your view, how likely or unlikely is it that a hung parliament would result in . . .

More moderate government

	1996
Very likely	15
Somewhat likely	34
Somewhat unlikely	18
Very unlikely	15
Don't know	18

Voices of the people

Weak and ineffective government

	%
Very likely	28
Somewhat likely	32
Somewhat unlikely	16
Very unlikely	9
Don't know	15

Uncertainty in financial markets

	%
Very likely	37
Somewhat likely	32
Somewhat unlikely	10
Very unlikely	5
Don't know	16

More considered legislation

	%
Very likely	16
Somewhat likely	32
Somewhat unlikely	16
Very unlikely	11
Don't know	25

Another general election within a year or so

	%
Very likely	48
Somewhat likely	31
Somewhat unlikely	6
Very unlikely	4
Don't know	11

Government listening to more voters

	%
Very likely	18
Somewhat likely	28
Somewhat unlikely	19
Very unlikely	21
Don't know	14

Table 54: What kind of government do people want?

How would you like the country to be governed: The largest party always forms a government on its own, even if the majority of people did not vote for it

	1998
Don't like it	33
Neutral	20
Like it	36
Don't know	12

Voices of the people

Governments require majority support, and hence usually involve a coalition of two or more parties

	1998
Don't like it	26
Neutral	20
Like it	43
Don't know	12

Governments are sometimes formed by a party with high support but not a majority, and sometimes formed by a coalition of parties with majority support

	1998
Don't like it	27
Neutral	22
Like it	37
Don't know	13

Source: MORI 1991; ICM 1996 and 1998

Devolution, pre-legislation

While some 60 per cent of respondents agree that government power in Britain is too centralised (see Table 8), there was a tendency in other responses to poll questions to prefer decision-making at national rather than regional or local level. Support for regional devolution in England has been lukewarm. In 1996, for example, more than half those interviewed thought educational standards should be set at national level and preferred a national strategy for planning and financing healthcare. People across Britain as a whole were generally supportive of Scottish devolution in the early 1990s, with Scotland remaining in the UK and having its own assembly with some taxation and spending powers. Only minorities of 5–10 per cent favoured a totally independent Scotland. The public were more ambivalent about devolution in Wales.

Table 55: Levels of governance (1996)

Some people feel that decisions are best made at national level, others argue for elected regional assemblies or local councils to play key roles. At what level should decisions be made on the following issues?

	National	Regional	Local
Developing major road and transport projects	39	38	23
Cleaning up rivers and beaches	38	35	28
Setting educational standards	56	23	21
Planning and financing healthcare	53	29	18
Attracting new investment and generating new jobs	41	38	22
Lobbying for EU regional funding	49	36	14

Table 56: Scottish devolution

Now thinking about the running of Scotland, which of these options would you most like to see?

	1991	1995
An independent Scotland, which is separate from both England and Wales and the European Community	10	5
An independent Scotland which is separate from England and Wales but part of the European Community	24	10
Scotland remaining part of the UK but with its own devolved assembly with some taxation and spending powers	46	50
No change from present system	16	24
Don't know	4	10

Voices of the people

Table 57: Referendum on Scottish assembly with tax and spending powers

Agreement with a proposal for a referendum in Scotland to decide on whether a Scottish assembly, with some taxation and spending powers, should be set up

	1995
Yes, hold	56
No, do not hold	24
Don't know	20

If there were a majority in Scotland in such a referendum for a Scottish assembly, with some taxation and spending powers, should Scotland be allowed one, or not?

	1995
Yes, should be allowed	69
No, should not be allowed	17
Don't know	14

Table 58: Welsh devolution

Would you support or oppose giving greater powers of government to Wales?

	1991	1995
Support	42	49
Oppose	40	34
Don't know	18	18

Table 59: Devolution to Northern Ireland

Would you support or oppose giving greater powers of government to Northern Ireland?

	1991	1995
Support	42	49
Oppose	43	32
Don't know	16	20

Table 60: Regional government in England

Would you support or oppose giving greater powers of government to regions, such as the West Country, North West, East Anglia, etc?

	1991	1995
Support	27	26
Oppose	61	60
Don't know	12	15

Table 61: Regional or national government in England?

Which of the following options do you prefer?

A   *People in this part of the country have particular social and economic interests that would be best served by an elected regional assembly*

B   *The people of the UK are best governed as a whole from Parliament*

	A Strongly agree/ Prefer	Neutral	B Strongly agree/ Prefer	Neutral
1995	37	19	38	6

Source: MORI 1991 and 1995; ICM 1996

Devolution, post-legislative opinion

By 2000, greater support for regional assemblies in England than in the 1990s seemed to be emerging. In the north of England, 43 per cent wanted an elected regional assembly to decide how to generate new jobs, develop major road and public transport and other similar issues, but devolutionary zeal was less evident elsewhere. In Scotland, London and Wales, respondents were in favour of giving devolved institutions more powers, overwhelmingly so in Scotland, but also in Wales and in London where nearly half the population advocated giving more policy-making powers to the London Mayor and Greater London Assembly.

Table 62: Giving people a choice on elected regional government in England

Agreement with the proposal that people in all areas of England should be given the opportunity to choose whether or not to have an elected regional assembly

	2000
Strongly agree	25
Tend to agree	31
Neither agree nor disagree	20
Tend to disagree	7
Strongly disagree	7
Don't know	11

Table 63: Choice between national, regional and local governance on selected issues (e.g., employment generation), England and by region

Thinking about England, which of the following options do you think is the best way of deciding how to generate new jobs, develop major road and public transport, and other similar issues?

	2000
Government ministers in Whitehall should decide, taking into account the needs of the country as a whole	12
An elected assembly for this region should decide	32
Government officials meeting at regional level should decide	15
Appointed businesses and local government representatives from this region should decide	29
Don't know	14

Preferences in the North between options for deciding how to generate new jobs, develop major road and public transport, and other similar issues

	%
Government ministers in Whitehall should decide, taking into account the needs of the country as a whole	16
An elected assembly for this region should decide	43
Government officials meeting at regional level should decide	9
Appointed businesses and local government representatives from this region should decide	15
Don't know	17

Voices of the people

Preferences in Yorkshire

	%
Government ministers in Whitehall should decide, taking into account the needs of the country as a whole	10
An elected assembly for this region should decide	34
Government officials meeting at regional level should decide	15
Appointed businesses and local government representatives from this region should decide	31
Don't know	11

Preferences in the East Midlands

	%
Government ministers in Whitehall should decide, taking into account the needs of the country as a whole	6
An elected assembly for this region should decide	24
Government officials meeting at regional level should decide	23
Appointed businesses and local government representatives from this region should decide	39
Don't know	9

Preferences in East Anglia

	%
Government ministers in Whitehall should decide, taking into account the needs of the country as a whole	12
An elected assembly for this region should decide	26
Government officials meeting at regional level should decide	24
Appointed businesses and local government representatives from this region should decide	29
Don't know	8

Preferences in the South East

	%
Government ministers in Whitehall should decide, taking into account the needs of the country as a whole	13
An elected assembly for this region should decide	34
Government officials meeting at regional level should decide	14
Appointed businesses and local government representatives from this region should decide	25
Don't know	15

Voices of the people

Preferences in the West Midlands

	%
Government ministers in Whitehall should decide, taking into account the needs of the country as a whole	11
An elected assembly for this region should decide	32
Government officials meeting at regional level should decide	15
Appointed businesses and local government representatives from this region should decide	28
Don't know	14

Preferences in the North West

	%
Government ministers in Whitehall should decide, taking into account the needs of the country as a whole	14
An elected assembly for this region should decide	26
Government officials meeting at regional level should decide	11
Appointed businesses and local government representatives from this region should decide	29
Don't know	21

Table 64: Who should make policy in London?

Thinking now about London, which of the following options do you think is the best way of deciding how to generate new jobs, develop major road and public transport, and other similar issues?

	%
Give more power to the London Mayor and Greater London Assembly	44
Keep the power of government ministers, Whitehall and the London Mayor and Greater London Assembly as they are now	37
Increase the power of government ministers and Whitehall	10
Don't know	9

Table 65: Who should make policy in Scotland?

Thinking now about Scotland, which of the following options do you think is the best way of deciding how to generate new jobs, develop major road and public transport, and other similar issues?

	%
Give more power to the Scottish Parliament and executive	72
Keep the power of government ministers, Whitehall and the Scottish Parliament and executive as they are now	20
Increase the power of government ministers and Whitehall	3
Don't know	6

Table 66: Who should make policy in Wales?

Thinking now about Wales, which of the following options do you think is the best way of deciding how to generate new jobs, develop major road and public transport, and other similar issues?

	%
Give more power to the Welsh National Assembly and executive	43
Keep the power of government ministers, Whitehall and the Scottish Parliament and executive as they are now	28
Increase the power of government ministers and Whitehall	10
Don't know	19

Source: ICM 2000

The civil service

Interviewing in 1996, we found strong support for greater openness and clearer lines of responsibilities for civil servants, with nearly nine out of ten agreeing that there should be a legal code of conduct defining civil servants' responsibilities. Three-quarters believed civil servants should be responsible to Parliament as well as to government ministers High levels felt that ministers should not be able to bar civil servants from giving evidence to a select committee or decide what evidence civil servants present to committees. There were concerns over the potential risks of civil servants exploiting their experience in government after taking up appointments in the private sector, and 70 per cent would have banned civil servants from taking jobs with companies they had dealt with within two years of leaving their official positions.

Table 67: Responsibilities of civil servants

To whom should civil servants be responsible?

	1996
Only to ministers, as now	18
Also directly to Parliament	75
Don't know	7

Should the responsibilities of civil servants be defined in a legal code of conduct?

	%
Yes	88
No	8
Don't know	4

Table 68: Civil service evidence to Parliament

Should ministers be able to decide what evidence civil servants give to select committees?

	1996
Yes	18
No	77
Don't know	5

Should ministers be able to bar civil servants, whom a committee wants to question, from giving evidence?

	%
Yes	18
No	79
Don't know	3

Voices of the people

Table 69: Civil service whistle-blowing

To whom should a civil servant who is aware that ministers or other officials are misleading Parliament be able to report his or her knowledge?

	2000
To his or her immediate superior, as now	27
To the chairman of the relevant Commons select committee	24
To the Speaker	43
Don't know	6
To Parliament (total)	67

Table 70: Post-service employment opportunities

Should civil servants be allowed to take jobs in companies they have dealt with as civil servants within two years of leaving their official positions?

	1995
Should	19
Should not	70
Don't know	11

Source: MORI 1995; ICM 1996.

The role of the judiciary

Asked about the powers of judges, respondents were clearly in favour of their scrutinising and regulating the activities of government ministers' with nearly four out of five agreeing that judges should use their powers to ensure government ministers act within the law.

Table 71: The use of judges' powers

Britain's judges have begun to use their powers more frequently to examine whether decisions taken by government ministers are legal or illegal. Could you tell me whether you agree or disagree with the following statements?

Judges now interfere too much in the decisions of government ministers

	1996
Agree	30
Disagree	43
Don't know	27

Judges must use their powers to ensure that government ministers act within the law

	1996
Agree	78
Disagree	10
Don't know	12

Judges nowadays provide a more effective check on government than MPs in Parliament do

	1996
Agree	39
Disagree	22
Don't know	40

Source: ICM 1996

Quangos

There is strong support for greater accountability and openness in both the appointment process to quangos and their activities. Respondents believed both the general public and Parliament should have access to more information about quangos. In 1995, 72 per cent of people wanted appointments of quango members to be subject to scrutiny by parliamentary committees. In the same year, 81 per cent wanted meetings and board papers to be available to the public. Most people preferred local elected or part-elected bodies to run local services, such as schools, further education, and health services, rather than appointed or self-appointing bodies as now. But there was considerable variation in people's preferences, depending on the local service and recent practice.

Table 72: Making quangos more accountable

Many important public services are now managed by 'quangos' – boards of people appointed by the government. For each of these statements about how services might be run in future, could you tell me to what extent you agree or disagree.

Government ministers should have the right to appoint whomever they think is most suitable to run quangos

	1995
Strongly agree	4
Tend to agree	22
Neither agree nor disagree	14
Tend to disagree	27
Strongly disagree	23
No opinion	10

All appointments to quangos should be subject to scrutiny by parliamentary committees

	%
Strongly agree	28
Tend to agree	44
Neither agree nor disagree	10
Tend to disagree	4
Strongly disagree	3
No opinion	11

Quangos should hold their board meetings in public and make all their board papers available to the public, subject to protection of commercial confidentiality and people's privacy

	%
Strongly agree	44
Tend to agree	37
Neither agree nor disagree	6
Tend to disagree	2
Strongly disagree	1
No opinion	10

There should be clear legal rules to ensure all quango boards are balanced in their composition

	%
Strongly agree	39
Tend to agree	41
Neither agree nor disagree	7
Tend to disagree	1
Strongly disagree	1
No opinion	10

Voices of the people

The general public should have a say in appointing some people to each quango

	%
Strongly agree	33
Tend to agree	38
Neither agree nor disagree	10
Tend to disagree	7
Strongly disagree	3
No opinion	10

Table 73: Who should run local services?

Which kind of organisation should run schools?

	1994
Local councils	38
Locally elected committees	26
Committees partly elected and partly appointed	13
Government-appointed committees	8
Self-appointing committees	8
Don't know	7

and further education?

	%
Local councils	35
Locally elected committees	18
Committees partly elected and partly appointed	15
Government-appointed committees	18
Self-appointing committees	7
Don't know	8

and hospitals?

	%
Local councils	27
Locally elected committees	23
Committees partly elected and partly appointed	18
Government-appointed committees	16
Self-appointing committees	8
Don't know	8

and police forces?

	%
Local councils	24
Locally elected committees	15
Committees partly elected and partly appointed	13
Government-appointed committees	37
Self-appointing committees	3
Don't know	9

and employment training?

	%
Local councils	30
Locally elected committees	19
Committees partly elected and partly appointed	11
Government-appointed committees	24
Self-appointing committees	5
Don't know	11

Voices of the people

and rented homes?

	%
Local councils	65
Locally elected committees	13
Committees partly elected and partly appointed	6
Government-appointed committees	5
Self-appointing committees	4
Don't know	8

and health authorities?

	1994*	2000
A committee of the local councils	30	8
A committee elected directly by local people	20	34
A committee which is partly elected, partly appointed	18	41
A government-appointed committee	20	11
Self-appointing committees	5	–
Don't know	8	7

*   The 1994 poll options were: local councils/locally elected committees/committees partly elected and partly appointed/government appointed committees/self-appointing committees/don't know.

Source: ICM for Channel 4 1994; MORI 1995

Freedom of Information

There has long been significant and growing enthusiasm for greater transparency and accessibility to the processes of government decision-making. As well as showing consensus-level support for a responsible Freedom of Information Act in general, the public are very much more radical in their views about the information which should be disclosed, with consensus around the desirability of disclosing cabinet and policy documents, and doing so either immediately or nearly so. There are also high levels of support for giving the Information Commissioner the final say on whether documents should be disclosed or kept secret.

Table 74: Support for a Freedom of Information Act

Agreement with the view that there should be a Freedom of Information Act in Britain, giving the right of access to information collected by public authorities, subject to adequate safeguards on national security, crime prevention and personal privacy

	1991	1995	1996	2000
Strongly agree	37	42	34	48
Tend to agree	40	39	43	31
Neither agree nor disagree	8	8	9	11
Tend to disagree	6	4	6	2
Strongly disagree	3	2	2	1
Don't know	5	4	5	7

Table 75: Release of cabinet and policy papers

Cabinet papers and papers used in government decision-making are kept secret for at least 30 years or more. Allowing for exemptions for national security and other significant matters, should any of the following categories of government papers be released earlier?

Background policy papers relating to government decisions

	1996
Yes	78
No	18
Don't know	4

Voices of the people

Civil service papers on government decisions

	%
Yes	78
No	17
Don't know	5

Cabinet papers

	%
Yes	74
No	20
Don't know	5

Table 76: How long should papers be kept secret?

How long should background policy papers relating to government decisions be kept secret?

	1996
For 20 years	4
For 10 years	26
Until after the next general election	21
For one year	12
Should be released immediately	34
Don't know	3

and civil servant advice papers on government decisions?

	%
For 20 years	2
For 10 years	23
Until after the next general election	21
For one year	14
Should be released immediately	38
Don't know	2

and cabinet papers?

	%
For 20 years	5
For 10 years	22
Until after the next general election	23
For one year	14
Should be released immediately	35
Don't know	2

Table 77: Policy advice: disclosure vs secrecy

Which of the following options do you prefer?

	2000
Policy advice from civil servants to ministers should normally be kept secret	17
Policy advice from civil servants to minister should normally be disclosed	68
Don't know	15

Table 78: Who should decide what official papers should be disclosed?

Parliament has been debating options for a new Freedom of Information Act. Which of the following options would you yourself prefer?

	2000
Ministers and civil servants should decide alone what government papers should be released	9
An independent commission should be able to order the release of government papers	79
Don't know	12

Under a new Freedom of Information Act, people can apply to get official information that would otherwise remain secret. Who should have the last word on whether this information is disclosed or kept secret?

	2001
Cabinet ministers	18
The new independent Information Commissioner	67
Don't know	16

Source: MORI 1991 and 1995; ICM 1996 and on the Scott inquiry 1996; ICM 2000 and 2001

Human rights

Prior to the Human Rights Act 2000, there was general agreement that citizens' rights were not well protected and that a Bill of Rights was necessary in Britain. Over 60 per cent of respondents did not trust governments with a large majority in Parliament to secure their rights. Asked what rights should be included in (or excluded from) a Bill of Rights, people showed a growing belief in all types of human right. The most popular item for a Bill of Rights was the right to hospital treatment on the NHS within a reasonable time; the second most popular right, supported by 93 per cent, was that of a fair trial before a jury. The least popular, at 66 per cent, was the right of a defendant to remain silent in court without prejudicing their case and a substantial minority opposed this item being included in a Bill of Rights. Questioned about police powers in 1997, responses were fairly evenly balanced about whether people should be penalised for remaining silent during police questioning. Respondents strongly disagreed with the proposal that the police should be able to search homes without a warrant (69 per cent) or question suspects for up to a week without letting them see a solicitor (85 per cent).

Table 79: Belief in a Bill of Rights

Agreement with the view that Britain needs a Bill of Rights to protect the liberty of the individual

	1991	1995	1996	2000
Strongly agree	31	34	30	39
Tend to agree	48	45	45	32
Neither agree nor disagree	10	11	11	13
Tend to disagree	5	6	6	4
Strongly disagree	1	2	2	3
Don't know/no opinion	5	3	6	9

Voices of the people

Table 80: Weakness of individual citizens' rights

Agreement with the view that British government can change individual citizens' rights too easily

	1991	1994	1995
Strongly agree	17	43	22
Tend to agree	37	29	41
Neither agree nor disagree	17	–	15
Tend to disagree	18	12	14
Strongly disagree	4	7	2
Don't know/no opinion	8	9	6

Table 81: Protection of rights in Europe and the UK

Individual citizens' rights are less well protected in Britain than in the rest of the European Community

	1991	1995
Strongly agree	12	16
Tend to agree	26	27
Neither agree nor disagree	23	23
Tend to disagree	20	16
Strongly disagree	4	4
Don't know/no opinion	16	15

Table 82: Political opinion as a safeguard of rights

In Britain, the rights of individual citizens are better protected by the force of political opinion than by formal legal safeguards

	1991	1995
Strongly agree	11	10
Tend to agree	37	32
Neither agree nor disagree	21	24
Tend to disagree	18	21
Strongly disagree	4	6
Don't know/no opinion	9	7

Table 83: Relying on politicians to protect rights

The good sense of elected politicians means a Bill of Rights isn't needed in Britain today

	1991	1995
Strongly agree	2	2
Tend to agree	9	15
Neither agree nor disagree	14	17
Tend to disagree	45	38
Strongly disagree	23	22
Don't know/no opinion	7	5

Voices of the people

Table 84: Danger to rights from large parliamentary majorities

Agreement with the view hat governments with a large majority in Parliament cannot always be trusted to respect our rights and liberties.

	1991	1995
Strongly agree	24	26
Tend to agree	46	48
Neither agree nor disagree	12	11
Tend to disagree	9	9
Strongly disagree	2	2
Don't know/no opinion	7	4

Table 85: What rights (from list) should be protected in a Bill of Rights?

	1991	1995	2000
Right to fair trial before a jury	77	82	93
Right of a woman to have an abortion	63	60	76
Right to join, or not to join, a trade union	75	71	87
Right of free assembly for peaceful meetings and demonstrations	56	59	86
Right to know what information government departments hold about you	75	74	89
Right to know the reasons for government decisions affecting you	–	–	90
Right of the press to report on matters of public interest	53	53	79
Right of British subjects to equal treatment on entering and leaving the UK, irrespective of colour or race	54	59	82

cont'd . . .

	1991	1995	2000
Right of those who are homeless to be housed	64	60	76
Right to hospital treatment on the NHS within a reasonable time	88	88	94
Right to privacy in your phone and mail communications	76	75	90
Right of privacy when you send or receive emails at home	–	–	83
Right to join a legal strike without losing your job	63	63	86
Right of a defendant to remain silent in court without prejudicing his case	40	32	66
Right to practise your religion without state interference	–	60	86
None of these	–	1	3
Don't know	–	2	1

Table 86: Which rights (from list) should not be protected in a Bill of Rights?

	1991	1995	2000
Right to fair trial before a jury	1	1	2
Right of a woman to have an abortion	11	10	13
Right to join, or not to join, a trade union	3	4	6
Right of free assembly for peaceful meetings and demonstrations	5	6	5
Right to know what information government departments hold about you	3	4	4
Right to know the reasons for government decisions affecting you	–	–	3

cont'd . . .

Voices of the people

	1991	1995	2000
Right of the press to report on matters of public interest	9	13	11
Right of British subjects to equal treatment on entering and leaving the UK, irrespective of colour or race	10	7	8
Right of those who are homeless to be housed	9	9	13
Right to hospital treatment on the NHS within a reasonable time	1	2	2
Right to privacy in your phone and mail communications	2	2	3
Right of privacy when you send or receive emails at home	–	–	6
Right to join a legal strike without losing your job	7	7	5
Right of a defendant to remain silent in court without prejudicing his case	17	29	20
Right to practise your religion without state interference	–	9	5
None of these	–	32	33
Don't know	–	13	22

Table 87: Police powers and the right of silence

Agreement with the statement that if someone remains silent during police questioning, it should count against them

	1997
Agree strongly	26
Agree	23
Disagree	26
Disagree strongly	21
Don't know	4

The police should NOT need a warrant to search the homes of suspects

	%
Agree strongly	15
Agree	14
Disagree	31
Disagree strongly	38
Don't know	2

The police should be allowed to question suspects for up to a week without letting them see a solicitor

	%
Agree strongly	7
Agree	6
Disagree	29
Disagree strongly	56
Don't know	2

Source: MORI 1991 and 1995; ICM for Channel 4 1994; ICM 1996, 1997 and 2000

Asylum policy

Respondents in 2000 were generally in favour of a 'case by case' approach to granting asylum to applicants for entry to the UK and opposed to a general presumption either that people would be either admitted or refused entry. Not surprisingly, respondents were most receptive to allowing entry to asylum-seekers who had a well-founded fear of death or torture in their own country or were fleeing from genocide or ethnic cleansing, and were least welcoming to those wanting to escape poverty in their own country. Thus, formally at least, respondents backed the government's avowed policy on asylum.

Table 88: Britain's approach to different categories of asylum-seekers

For these different categories of asylum-seekers, should we usually allow entry into the UK, usually refuse entry, or judge each case on its merits?

People who want to escape poverty in their own country

	2000
Usually allow entry	13
Usually refuse entry	34
Judge each case on its merits	48
Don't know	5

People who have a well-founded fear of death or torture in their own country

	%
Usually allow entry	40
Usually refuse entry	14
Judge each case on its merits	42
Don't know	4

People who are fleeing civil war or armed invasion in their own country

	%
Usually allow entry	30
Usually refuse entry	19
Judge each case on its merits	46
Don't know	5

People who have suffered political repression or persecution in their own country

	%
Usually allow entry	29
Usually refuse entry	19
Judge each case on its merits	48
Don't know	5

People who are fleeing from genocide or ethnic cleansing

	%
Usually allow entry	40
Usually refuse entry	13
Judge each case on its merits	42
Don't know	5

Source: ICM 2000

Popular protest

The year 2000 saw an outbreak of popular protest, including petrol blockades in Britain by road hauliers and farmers. Nearly half the population thought the blockades were 'justified', and a further 29 per cent believed they were 'perhaps justified' (74 per cent in total). More than half the respondents also took a benign view of the French port blockades. Of other protests. the street demonstrations against capitalism in London and the demonstrations at the world trade talks in Seattle and Prague were the least supported (although the number of respondents regarding them as 'definitely' or 'perhaps' justified outnumbered those who did not). Overall, just about half the respondents believed that protests, blockades and demonstrations were a legitimate way of expressing people's concerns, and were divided over whether governments should change their policies in response to protests, with 39 per cent saying they should and 35 per cent that they should not.

Table 89: What kinds of protest are justifiable? (2000)

Some people have been discussing recently what kinds of protests are justifiable in a democracy. For each of the following protests, please say whether you think they were definitely justified, perhaps justified, perhaps not justified or definitely not justified?

Street demonstrations against capitalism in London

	Total	England	London	Scotland	Wales
Definitely justified	18	19	9	19	16
Perhaps justified	29	29	22	34	34
Perhaps not justified	18	17	26	14	17
Definitely not justified	24	22	36	23	20
Don't know	11	12	7	10	14

Countryside Alliance and pro-hunting demonstrations

	Total	England	London	Scotland	Wales
Definitely justified	27	29	18	25	25
Perhaps justified	28	27	31	32	29
Perhaps not justified	15	15	17	14	14
Definitely not justified	22	21	24	23	26
Don't know	8	8	10	6	6

The destruction of genetically modified (GM) crops in government-approved trials

	Total	England	London	Scotland	Wales
Definitely justified	28	28	25	29	22
Perhaps justified	27	28	26	27	28
Perhaps not justified	17	16	21	18	22
Definitely not justified	18	19	16	19	17
Don't know	10	10	11	7	10

French blockades at ports over petrol

	Total	England	London	Scotland	Wales
Definitely justified	28	28	17	29	41
Perhaps justified	25	26	17	25	30
Perhaps not justified	16	15	24	13	11
Definitely not justified	25	25	29	26	15
Don't know	6	6	13	7	3

Voices of the people

The petrol blockades here by some road hauliers and farmers

	Total	England	London	Scotland	Wales
Definitely justified	45	46	35	48	61
Perhaps justified	29	28	33	30	26
Perhaps not justified	9	9	13	9	6
Definitely not justified	13	13	16	10	6
Don't know	4	4	2	3	1

The demonstrations at the world trade talks in Seattle and Prague

	Total	England	London	Scotland	Wales
Definitely justified	16	18	11	16	9
Perhaps justified	26	26	24	27	33
Perhaps not justified	13	13	19	11	14
Definitely not justified	14	13	16	16	14
Don't know	30	30	30	31	31

Table 90: Are protests a legitimate way of expressing popular concerns? (2000)

Agreement with the view that if governments don't listen, peaceful protest, blockades and demonstrations are a legitimate way of expressing people's concerns

	Total	England	London	Scotland	Wales
Strongly agree	49	48	38	57	62
Tend to agree	32	33	39	28	24
Neither agree nor disagree	8	9	10	5	6
Tend to disagree	4	4	6	4	3
Strongly disagree	3	3	6	2	4
Don't know	4	4	1	4	1

Table 91: How should governments respond to protests?

In a parliamentary democracy, governments should not change policies in response to protests, blockades or demonstrations

	Total	England	London	Scotland	Wales
Strongly agree	13	14	10	8	11
Tend to agree	22	23	19	18	17
Neither agree nor disagree	19	19	12	15	16
Tend to disagree	23	22	35	26	27
Strongly disagree	16	15	24	25	19
Don't know	7	7	1	8	9

Source: ICM 2000

The National Health Service

The 2000 poll, carried out before the new National Plan for the NHS was unveiled, indicated that the public wished for increased public consultation and a clear constitution for the NHS defining the government's obligation to provide free medical care at the time of need. Compared to the 55 per cent of respondents who thought they should have a lot of power over the medical treatment they received on the NHS, only 20 per cent believed that they actually did so.

Voices of the people

Table 92: Giving the NHS a constitution of its own

Which of the following comes closest to your view?

	2000
The NHS needs a constitution of its own to define the government's duty to deliver free medical care at a time when people require it	69
The public should trust elected politicians in government to safeguard the NHS's performance of its duty to the public	26
Don't know/not sure	5

Table 93: How open and consultative is the NHS?

Thinking about the way the NHS responds to the public and users of its services, which comes closest to your view?

	2000
The NHS is run in an open way and consults the public	36
The NHS is remote from the public and is hard to influence	56
Don't know	8

Table 94: Patients' power over medical treatment

Thinking about the medical treatment that you or members of your family have received under the National Health Service, would you say that you had . . .

	2000
A lot of power over how you were treated	20
A little power over how you were treated	51
No power at all over how you were treated	22
Don't know/not sure	7

How much power do you think that you and other patients should have over medical treatment?

	2000
A lot of power	55
A little power	39
No power	3
Don't know/not sure	4

Source: ICM for the Hutton Commission (funded by JRRT) 2000

European integration

In the early to mid-1990s, the Rowntree Trust wished to poll heavily on possible developments within the European Union and the public's responses to these developments. The tables below indicate a gradual shift against the European project. In 1991, 43 per cent stated that economic and political union with Europe would strengthen Britain's ability to protect its interests, compared to 31 per cent who thought it would weaken them. By 1995, however, opinion had shifted in the opposite direction. Marginally more people (37 per cent) believed the EU weakened Britain's ability to protect its interests than the 32 per cent who believed it strengthened them.

Nearly 60 per cent wanted a referendum on the decision on joining the single currency and nearly half wanted a referendum on EU membership. In 1996, a quarter of those responding believed that joining the single currency would be 'very bad' – twice as many who thought it would be 'very good'.

Voices of the people

Table 95

Which of the following options do you prefer?

A *Moves towards economic and political union with Europe will weaken Britain's ability to protect British interests by handing power to Europe*

B *Moves towards economic and political union with Europe will strengthen Britain's ability to protect British interests by gaining collective power*

	A Strongly agree/ Prefer	Neutral	B Strongly agree/ Prefer	Neutral
1991	31	21	43	6
1995	37	23	32	7

Table 96: Predictions on developments in the EU (1991)

From this list of possible developments from closer government co-ordination in the European Community, which do you think are likely to happen in the next ten years?

	1991
A single European currency	56
A common European defence policy	42
Improvements in workers' rights	33
Freedom to work in any member state	53
Cleaner beaches	44
Laws which are less sensitive to the British way of life	33
More individual liberties than we have now	19
Better ability to deal with terrorism	35
A different electoral system	27
A higher standard of living	30
None of these	1
Don't know/no opinion	9